DEFENSE WITH A KNIFE

DEFENSE WITH A KNIFE

FLORIAN LAHNER

SCHIFFER MILITARY
4880 Lower Valley Road | Atglen, PA 19310

Library of Congress Control Number: 2018957976

Cover design by Justin Watkinson
Book design by Jack Chappell
Type set in Transformers/Times New Roman

ISBN: 978-0-7643-5677-3
Printed in China

Published by Schiffer Publishing, Ltd.
4880 Lower Valley Road
Atglen, PA 19310
Phone: (610) 593-1777; Fax: (610) 593-2002
E-mail: Info@schifferbooks.com
Web: www.schifferbooks.com

For our complete selection of fine books on this and related subjects, please visit our website at www.schifferbooks.com. You may also write for a free catalog.

Schiffer Publishing's titles are available at special discounts for bulk purchases for sales promotions or premiums. Special editions, including personalized covers, corporate imprints, and excerpts, can be created in large quantities for special needs. For more information, contact the publisher.

We are always looking for people to write books on new and related subjects. If you have an idea for a book, please contact us at proposals@schifferbooks.com.

Disclaimer: All techniques and exercises shown and described in this book were presented by the author and publisher according to the best of their knowledge and belief. But neither the publisher nor the author can assume any liability for possible accidents or injuries that may occur during practice.

Life is modular.
It's just a matter of perspective.

CONTENTS

ACKNOWLEDGMENTS

Thanks to Karl Heinz Schnurrer for his generous help as my partner during the photo shoots, Frank Soens and his assistant for the good and relaxed atmosphere during the shooting and for the great photos.

Special thanks to all the teachers and students who gave me insight into their knowledge.

I say thanks to my big brother and teacher Bram Frank, who took me into his family. His system and way of teaching gave me greater access to martial arts and more insights into defense systems than I had ever thought possible. Moreover, with his contribution to what is best described by the term "combat arts," he gave me real perspectives for realistic use. This is a goal that many systems promise, but only few achieve.

FOREWORD

The best thing for a teacher is to see how his or her own students turn into teachers themselves. This relates to the job of being a teacher and is similar to the role of parents. A child succeeds in the same field of endeavor as the parents; in this special case, it is even better. I could not think of any more of an apt student, and I see Florian rather as my son or younger brother. You can bet that I am very proud of him. And it is an honor for me to write the preface for his long-expected first book.

We speak different languages and stem from different cultures and continents but are nevertheless as close to each other as almost nobody else. Why? Because we are connected by martial arts and personal combat training. It is said that a teacher appears just at the right moment in life. This was the case for me with respect to the late professor Remy Presas, the founder of the Philippine martial art of Modern Arnis. He taught me the martial art of his ancestors and encouraged me to become a master of the blade.

When the time arrived for Florian, I appeared in his life. And I am very grateful for that! Florian absorbed what I taught and turned it into something really original. He flourished with the Common Sense Self Defense (CSSD) concept systems. In his teaching and his actions I can recognize myself.

Florian had so much respect that I literally had to push him out of the nest and reassure him that some fame is not only acceptable, but even necessary. It is an honor for me that he stepped into the limelight: there he shows his understanding of the CSSD modular system and the seamless change from the very calm Florian into something I personally call the "Dr. Destructo" mode. Here he teaches at the highest level and is able to flesh out his teachings with real, true application.

What does all this have to do with the book you have in front of you? Everything! This book is a treasure, a codex for understanding the Modular System and its relation to our tool, the knife. One of its best representatives and teachers, Florian Lahner, shows how easy it is in practice. You don't have to be a genius to be proficient in CSSD/SC! Florian has influenced my life, and with his book he will also influence yours.

Bram Frank
Founder of Common Sense
Self Defense / Street Combat

INTRODUCTION

This book deals with the use of knives for self-defense. You can see that this is no easy topic, because almost nothing has been published with respect to this. Anybody engaging in self-defense realizes that they have to fight their way through an almost impenetrable jungle of different systems. It starts with traditional styles and ends with modern hybrid systems, all of which promise to be the best solution to attacks of any kind.

But defense is a lot more than just physical arguments. It includes knowledge about the structure of conflicts, psychological aspects, but also the choice of tools and weapons.

Yes. You did read it right. Defense can and has to use auxiliary means, should the situation arise, in order to compensate for disadvantages by surprise, physical factors, or being outnumbered. In this book I introduce the knife as one of the most effective weapons at close range. You will come to know a system clearly distinct from "stabbings" and teaching a responsible use of blades. You will see that this does not happen at the expense of effectiveness.

After long years of training in various systems, I came to the realization that I did not have any really good concepts at hand against knife attacks. On the search for solutions I was lucky to meet the American Bram Frank. I learned the use of blades and their inherent dangers. The old proverb came true: I met my teacher at exactly the time I was ready for him. Bram Frank's "Modular System" is intriguingly simple and logical, and this is also its strength. Suddenly, I had a system at hand in which I could have real confidence that it could be effectively used.

Neither acrobatic jumps nor complicated combinations of technique lead to success: "Combat must be simple" is one of Bram Frank's guidelines. "Simple" sounds good, doesn't it? I am sure you can do this as well!

Florian Lahner

An Important Note

This book ought to give insight into defense with blades. It neither can nor should replace training under professional supervision. First, read the entire book and try to imagine the entire series of images. Not everything may be immediately clear to you. Don't worry, "learning by doing" is what is asked for.

As the next step, imitate the movements shown in each image together with a partner. Use only suitable training knives and protect yourself—especially your eyes! Train in a controlled way and beware of overeagerness, which causes injuries. Train regularly, with high rates of repetition. This is the only way to train your reflexes.

Defense is not only a matter of techniques. A legal and ethical response depends on many factors. The most important one: if possible, avoid any physical confrontation and already think of the consequences of your actions beforehand.

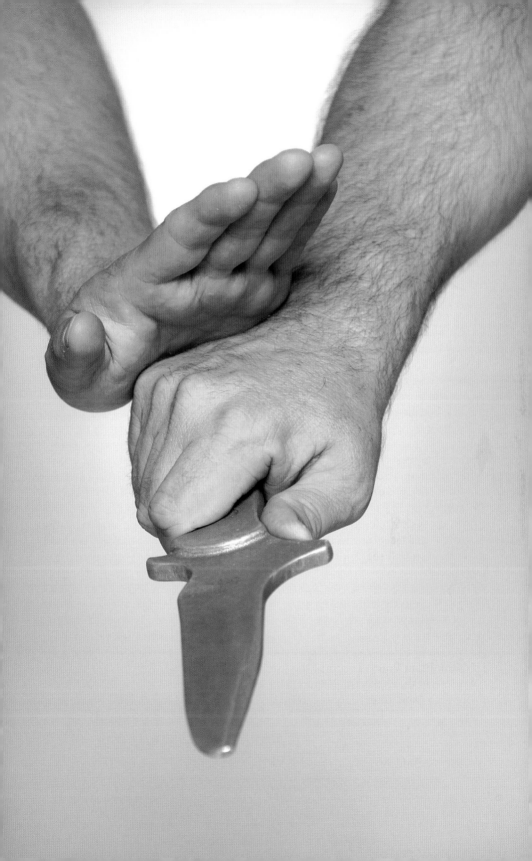

CHAPTER ONE
THE KNIFE AS A WEAPON FOR DEFENSE

The history of the use of tools is as old as humanity. Archeological finds provide information about the degree of development of a society by means of their tools and the varieties of these implements. One of the oldest auxiliary means of humans is the blade, regardless of whether it is made of stone, bronze, or high-performance steel. Whenever a task was at hand that was beyond the physical capabilities of humans, they invented and used a suitable tool. The blade represents a typical example of the ingenuity of mankind.

As old as the history of humanity is the history of their conflicts, and these too were carried out with tools. While instruments for hitting, such as the club, were still dependent on the force of their user, blades allowed even weak and physically inferior humans to defend themselves. This is still valid today.

Most self-defense systems are dedicated to fighting without weapons. The intrepid hero in his conspicuous white

Edged weapons have been aiding humans and their predecessors since prehistoric times.

outfit survives, at least in the imagination of many trainers, against whole hordes of heavily armed attackers. Hollywood contributed its part to this image. Almost always the hero bashes to victory and wins his true love by using only his fists and feet. The baddies, in turn, are easily recognized by their long knives.

There are at least social and historical reasons for this. While swords in Europe are usually a symbol for nobility and the government's lordship, the knife-wielding bandit could always be found in stories. When you put aside these clichés, you will find that knives are very effective and simple tools for self-defense.

A tool for self-defense? This idea surely will make some established "self-defense experts" faint. But you have to realize what self-defense is: defending against an attack on your physical integrity, or defense against severe injuries, threats, or mortal dangers.

Contrary to the often somewhat romantic ideas of many martial artists and trainers, a defensive situation is very complex and not so easy to handle. Many factors contribute to this. First of all, you should let go of the thought that all criminals are totally "dim." Studies have shown quite clearly that violent criminals are very "qualified" for their job. As perpetrators they have a very fine feel for potential victims and the best opportunities for performing their deeds. Thus you have to assume that the perpetrators usually have all advantages on their side, because only they can determine the time and place of the attack. In addition, they are sure that the deed will be a pushover, which means that they are physically superior and will use a weapon, if necessary. In many cases perpetrators are not alone, which additionally lessens your chance of successful resistance.

Whoever still believes that only "harmless brawls" exist should study the newspapers of a single week. Without having to get into the well-known attempts at explanation, such as the brutalization of society or the consequences of television consumption and of violent gaming, it can be shown with statistics that violence is an everyday issue.

And not only this—violence has also become less scrupulous and more destructive. The use of weapons (bottles, sticks, knives) during physical arguments is increasing. People lying on the ground are kicked until they are half dead. Whoever thinks he or she will lose draws a knife and stabs. With knives and even firearms, brand-name clothes and money are "withdrawn"; victims are bullied or brought under one's control by the force of weapons and then tortured.

These are not paranoid scenarios, but everyday examples I have seen myself: the victims whom I have met on the job, and the experiences I have been told about by the participants in seminars. Attacks with weapons are everyday issues, which can also be seen in the daily routines in hospitals.

Weaponless self-defense systems usually have in common that they practice constructed situations that don't even rudimentarily contain the kinds of brutality and threat that actual perpetrators display every day. In brief: the training is not for reality. Self-defense courses for women, too, quite often share this problem because they practice cliché situations that don't

have anything in common with the dramatic course of an actual assault.

I don't think it's a good idea to base defense practice on internet wisdom, clichés, or hearsay. This can have fatal consequences, but unfortunately it is often managed this way. Don't let yourself be deceived by such, and, above all, don't believe everything you can read on the internet. Blindly following pithy sayings won't protect you. For practice it is better to follow reliable sources.

Real situations with all disadvantages on the side of the defender can't be solved with fists alone. Fair play, even chances, and rules are available only in sports, but

In common perception, knives are often seen in the hands of malicious baddies only. Whoever accepts this view only limits himself or herself in their possibilities.

there are also weight categories and referees. These don't exist in a defense situation. What's left is to compensate for your weaknesses and disadvantages, and this can be done with the best prospects for success by using tools. In particular, knives—if legal under the circumstances—are very well suited for defense.

Ontario Knives' RAT3 is an outstanding all-purpose knife, developed in cooperation with Randall's Adventure & Training Team. For many people, the handle is a bit too short, but you ought to shortlist it in any case.

Ontario Knives' Abaniko Tactical Knife, designed by Bram Frank. The knife, available in a 5-inch or 7-inch version, rests extremely comfortably in your hand and allows a multitude of uses. In Germany, it can't be carried for civil defense, and it is extremely large for everyday use. For professional users, this would be my first choice.

Every chandler praises his candles, but here the praise is based on firm conviction: the Wa2Go (Way to Go) by Florian Lahner. This is a comfortable small knife with the best handle properties and is an extremely good tool knife for all purposes. Here, the prototype of the model in the Böker Plus series.

CHAPTER TWO

FACTORS BELOW THE LEVEL OF PHYSICAL VIOLENCE

It would be wrong to reduce a situation of self-defense to the bare physical violence. Too many factors play a role in the course of the conflict. Quite often these factors are decisive for the outcome of the situation. Thus a closer look pays off.

2.1 PREVENTION

The most sensible defense against any kind of attack is "Don't be there!," meaning just don't be at the place where the trouble is.

Regardless of how much training and time you have invested in your ability to defend yourself, sometimes you're unlucky, somebody else is lucky, or somewhere there is somebody better than you. The best practice is that you avoid, in general, places and situations where quarrel and escalation may occur. Only few people necessarily have to walk through the roughest quarter of the town at two o'clock in the morning. The price for a taxi is lower—especially when shared with friends—than the results of a violent encounter.

Of course, you should not start any kind of provocation. It doesn't pay to utter your displeasure about something if the payback is the threat of injuries or worse. A part of successful defense is not to give in to childish provocations and not to think further about any verbal insult. Many potential perpetrators try to seduce the victim into making an attack so that they have a "justification" for violent acts. Whoever doesn't fall for this has already partly won.

Here, too, it is important to recognize potential conflicts or dicey situations in advance. With a bit of attention this can be done in many cases. For this you need a certain willingness to perceive your surroundings. Whoever walks through the streets at night, with loud music in their ears while staring at their mobile phone, doesn't need to wonder if they suddenly find themselves amid a group of mobbing drunkards. Probably alone, too, because all other pedestrians have already seen and heard this group from afar.

Being vigilant in order to avoid conflicts is an important part of self-defense discipline. The following questions are helpful:

Are the surroundings suitable for an attack? (ambush)
Where would I start an attack?
Is there enough space for dodging?
Are there other pedestrians and would an attack raise too much attention?
Do any persons show suspicious behavior (look around very often or point at me)?
Am I being followed? (cross to the other side of the street a couple of times to find out)
Am I a stranger here and look like one to others?

Active preparation helps with prevention (e.g., it is good to match clothing and shoes to your defense capabilities). Women, for example, can put on sport shoes after the disco or party. If you carry a tool for self-defense, your clothing has to allow quick access. If you have a flashlight with you, dark places are less problematic because orientation and identifying a definite target are easier. Powerful flashlights, in addition, allow blinding and diverting the attacker or can be used as a tool for hitting.

Unknown stretches to navigate can contain especially many dangers because you know neither the area nor alternate routes or possibilities of escape. In addition, you pay less attention to your defense because your head is occupied with orientation. Thus, if necessary, you should explore a new stretch of terrain during daylight (e.g., with your car and without deadline pressure).

2.2. PRECONFLICT PHASE

If a confrontation can't be avoided, what will happen is nevertheless open. Only few attacks in the civilian realm occur without warning; a real ambush, rather, happens in a military context. In the preconflict phase the switches are already set for the later course of action. Normal citizens are involved in encounters as an effect of rude behavior or as a target of mugging. If a conflict can't be avoided, there are still many possibilities to influence the course of action prior to an attack on your body.

Prohibited items are explicitly mentioned in the law, such as the brass knuckles and balisong shown here. Often they represent strange status symbols. But any good kitchen knife is more dangerous.

Secure hold of the flashlight with blinding

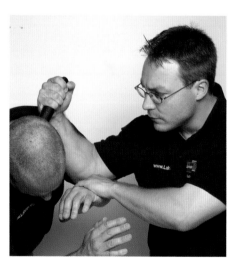

Baton technique with the flashlight

2.2.1. DISTANCE

Under all circumstances, keep your distance to the attacker as large as possible. This gives you more time to react to attacks because the attacker first has to cross that distance before reaching you with his extremities or weapons. While he or she is approaching, you can enlarge the distance again or start a counterattack.

But all theory assumes ideal circumstances, because quite often the distance can't be chosen at will (e.g., in crowded discos, narrow hallways or public traffic). In these cases, obstacles that you put between yourself and the attacker can impede his way and give you a temporary advantage. Tables, pushed-over chairs, or traffic signs constrain the attacker to follow circular paths and give an advantage to you.

2.2.2. DE-ESCALATION

Another important aspect of the preconflict phase is de-escalation. Body language and nonverbal communication are used both by the attacker and the defender. The roles of perpetrator and victim are first defined by the offender. He poses in front of you, large and threatening, and shows with all kinds of signals that he is the more powerful. Here it is important to know that the roles of perpetrator and victim mutually cause each other. If he is the perpetrator, then you are necessarily the victim. This is the same as yin and yang in Asian philosophy, which together create a full circle as two opposing parts requiring each other.

If you are becoming a victim, you signal this by sagging shoulders, lowering your eyes, talking in an uncertain voice, and receding. Many people don't know how to react and become ever smaller, smile uncertainly, and agree to all accusations and threats of the attacker. This inevitably results in the attacker being reassured in his behavior and ramping up ever more until the violence starts.

Auxiliary means are always the preferred choice for defense. Here, creating distance by means of a chair.

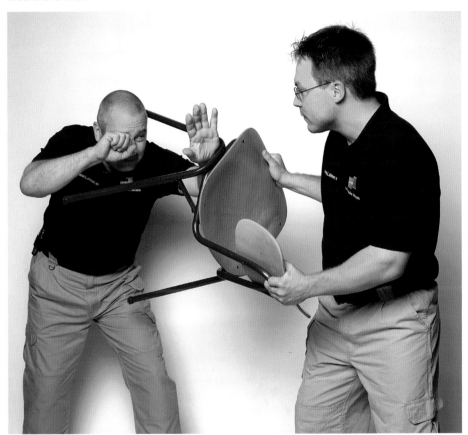

This is no wonder, since we are no longer used to direct violence in our society. We let ourselves be impressed by humans who put themselves outside any rules, because only few of us have ever learned how to deal with such situations.

During our education and socialization we have learned to stick to rules. If these rules were broken by others, there was always an institution we could call on. This way, either the teacher, the parent, or the police took care that the rules were reinstated.

But in an immediately threatening confrontation these institutions are not at our disposal. Here, I want to explicitly point out that neither the surrounding pedestrians nor friends nor an emergency call can prevent escalation. Cases where the entirety of passengers in a subway compartment watched or looked away without helping, the friends suddenly vanished, or the police showed up only when the victim was already lying on the ground and the perpetrator had disappeared are common occurrences.

How should you behave? Demonstrate your strength! Why should you be the victim? If you don't act like a victim, then the other person can't be a perpetrator. Assume a stable and secure stance. This means that your feet are about a shoulder's width apart, with one foot in front of the other. Bend your knees a bit. The weight on your legs should be either evenly distributed or slightly on the rear leg (to about 60 percent). This allows for a stable stance, while you are nevertheless able to dodge quick movements or to counterattack. Turn one shoulder slightly toward the attacker so as not to offer him your entire front. Lift your arms and turn your palms toward the attacker.

By this, you signal the following: first, the stable stance appears calm, secure, and not fearful. The open hands at the same time show willingness for open communication but also mark the perimeter of a security area and make it clear: "Stop! Don't come closer!"

At the same time, you have the possibility to start an aggressive counterattack from this position with only minimal change of your posture by gliding forward and putting your weight onto the leg in front. If this security area is crossed, push straight ahead with the heel of your frontal hand. Depending on the situation, this can also be a warning (the target here is the attacker's breastbone). When pushing forward, put your entire weight into it (without losing your balance).

The posture achieved in this way can thus appear to be calming, nonaggressive, and self-confident, but at the same time it gives you the chance to actively get the situation under control. From here you can start de-escalation. Try to judge the attacker's intentions. Does he want to let steam off or is this a mugging? Can you clear the situation without using force?

It is important to appear clear headed, transparent, and self-confident. I don't recommend doing whatever the attacker wants without any limits in order to get away without a scratch. There are several reasons

A defensive stance that is at the same time calming and open

for this, the most important being that he may execute his plan regardless of what you are doing. Appeals to reason or pledges are not only useless but confirm to him his position of strength, which he will then build up even more, because for him it is all about power games and demonstrations of his own power. This is valid for sexual attacks as well as verbal assaults or physical attacks.

In some situations it can be helpful to play along in pretense. At the time the attacker feels himself assured in his position, your defense hits him all the more surprisingly. But for this you have to be sure not to become totally paralyzed by his superiority, like a rabbit staring at a snake.

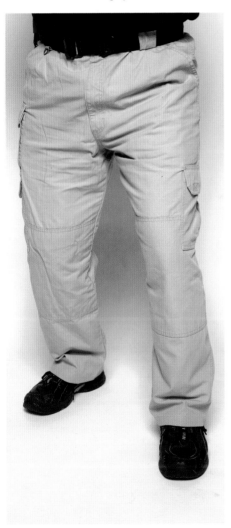

Stable and natural stance with feet a shoulder's width apart

Defensive posture seen from the side. The hands are approximately level with the face.

You will have greatest success if you don't allow the consolidation of the attacker's position of power. Thus, set clear limits for the attacker but also for yourself. Later on in this book, when we will deal with using knives for self-defense against attacks with deadly intent, this aspect is especially important. There has to be a clear point for you when you are ready to escalate too. Hesitation as well as rash action leads to even-more-complicated situations.

Another reason for not doing what is expected of you: only if you display self-assured behavior can you de-escalate from a position of power. You should not beg for a peaceful solution but should offer this option from a position of strength. Part of this is not to drive the attacker into a corner. Don't engage in word fights and insults. Make your point as clearly and simply as possible. Only then can it be understood and followed by your opponent while being stressed. Insults compel the other person to actions. You should be above this.

Chances for getting injured in a confrontation (with weapons) are high. So

Push with the ball of the hand toward the bottom of the nose. The rear hand still provides cover.

Starting position. Keep in mind to make the distance to the attacker as far away as possible in a real situation.

The neutral starting position. The weight is about evenly distributed on both legs.

22

why should you get into this risk because of a verbal insult? Only if you are ready to defend yourself can you be generous here. Something that acts like a miracle time and again is to say, "I'm sorry that I bumped into you inadvertently. I'll buy you a drink. Will everything be all right again afterward?"

2.2.3. INVOLVING WITNESSES

Your demonstratively displayed calmness and lack of aggression in gestures and words have an additional purpose: to include passersby and possible witnesses. I don't believe that a confrontation with weapons will stay unnoticed and uninvestigated. During my talks with them, in-the-know government officials and policemen who are among my students have clearly indicated that one should count on being investigated as a participant. I believe that

Push with the ball of the hand as a stop or light counterattack.

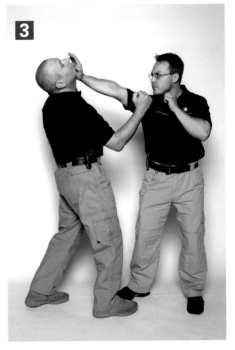

Push with the ball of the hand toward the underside of the chin. The entire body follows the head after impact; thus, this may lead to a backward fall.

A view of the situation just prior to escalation

4

A determined counter-attack uses the shifting of weight toward the opponent.

quickly vanishing from the scene in combination with getting rid of the weapon and other such reflexive actions is criminal and also unfavorable with respect to further consequences. But more on that later.

Make it clear to all surrounding people that you are not asking for trouble, but that in contrast this is the attacker's intention. Use the just-described hand position to convince others of your peacefulness. Lift your hands to protect yourself or for calming down; both allow a counterattack at any time. But those who are in the sur-

rounding area will recognize that you are the victim. Support this by shouting "Go away! I don't want any quarrel!"

Turn to a specific bystander. "You, the one with the blue jacket! I am being attacked by this man. Please, call the police!" Only if you order somebody specifically do you involve this person in the action. All the passersby would love to watch the action, but actually nobody wants to have anything to do with it. In addition, there are still helpful humans who don't dare to do anything, partly because they don't know what has to be done and partly because they don't want to stand out from the anonymous mass. If you talk directly to individuals, you relieve them from the decision of what has to be done.

Point out the attacker's course of action: "He has a knife! He wants to stab me!" This all serves to isolate the attacker (also from his buddies) and also makes your situation clear to the witnesses, with only little leeway for misinterpretation.

2.3. CONFLICT PHASE

If there is a fight despite of all your efforts, you should end it as quickly as possible without any risk to yourself and in accordance with the law. Act with determination but without unnecessary brutality. This book is about how to do this even in life-threatening situations. More about this in chapter 4.

2.4. POSTCONFLICT PHASE

What happens right after the—successful—fight? Not much can be found about this in the literature, and this is trained even less. Nevertheless, this is almost as important as the actions prior to the fight and the fight itself. After successfully stopping the attack, you are probably filled with adrenaline, are shaking like crazy, and are unable to have any clear thoughts. Therefore it is especially important to practice this situation too. First of all, you should assure yourself that no further dangers are coming from the attacker. Can you see him? Is he running away? Is he lying on the ground? Do you secure him there or is he lying without moving? Do you see his hands and are they without weapons?

5

The counterattack was primarily successful and the attacker went down.

2.4.1. THE 360° CHECK

Now, you check the full circle around you. An attacker is rarely alone, and the chances that his buddy just hits you from behind with his baseball bat are high. Get used to a close-combat routine to avoid mistakes and stay capable of acting under stress. Thus, first check the success of your defense on the opponent, localize him, and make sure that he is no longer posing a danger.

Afterward, scan your surroundings to the left and right. Is there help available for you, or more potential opponents? Last (this is often forgotten), turn around completely and look behind. How is the situation there?

Then turn toward a better position. Get some distance from the attacker and position yourself in a way that gives you a good overview of everything and enables

you to see further attackers from afar. If possible, place some obstacles into a potential path of attack.

You should enhance your situation as quickly as possible during these actions by taking a tool for defense into your hands, be it an umbrella, a key, irritant gas, a knife, or some kind of operating resources. Now you call for help by talking to a passerby or making an emergency call.

2.4.2. SELF-EXAMINATION

Because you are pumped up with adrenaline, you may have overlooked any injuries until now. This may sound strange but can be seen time and again. In particular, stabs with edged weapons and even injuries from firearms are often overlooked at the be-

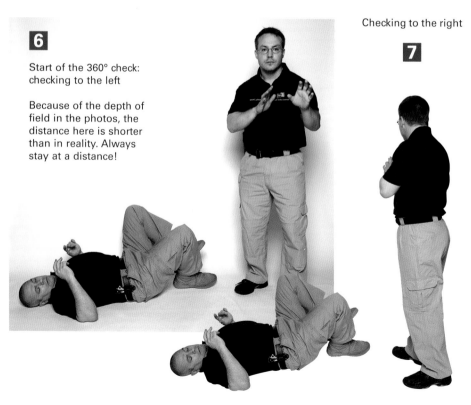

Checking to the right

6

Start of the 360° check: checking to the left

Because of the depth of field in the photos, the distance here is shorter than in reality. Always stay at a distance!

7

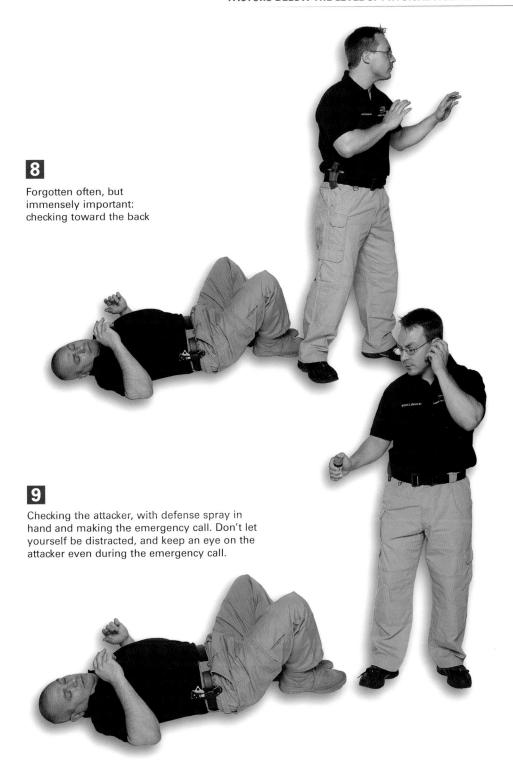

8

Forgotten often, but immensely important: checking toward the back

9

Checking the attacker, with defense spray in hand and making the emergency call. Don't let yourself be distracted, and keep an eye on the attacker even during the emergency call.

ginning. But your organism becomes weakened, and you surely don't want to flake out when the buddies of the attacker appear, do you?

Thus, inspect yourself thoroughly for injuries. Move your hand over your chest, belly, neck, head, face, arms, and legs. Also try to inspect your back as much as possible, especially the area around the kidneys. In principle, you move your hands all over your body without leaving gaps, as if you wanted to soap yourself under the shower. This way you check all the body regions. Do this systematically so as not to leave out any part of the body.

2.4.3. STOPPING BLEEDING

If you see blood, investigate whether you can stop the bleeding. To do this, you use specific points on your body at which applied pressure can stop the blood flow through the arteries toward the bleeding. Of course, this book is no first-aid course, but maybe it will inspire you to deal with this topic again.

For training, you can ask a partner to check whether the extremities (this means fingers and toes) after the pressure point are getting paler or whether the pulse is weakening or even missing. If this is the case, you have done everything right.

Self-examination for injuries: skull, chest and belly, lower abdomen, and genitals

Kidney area

Arms

Thighs

Lower Legs

2.4.4. SHOCK POSITION

If you can't stop the bleeding or have already lost a lot of blood, lie on the ground and be sure that your head is the lowest point of your body. This is the shock position, as you know from a first-aid course. Legs up alone doesn't help! It is imperative that all available blood reaches the head. This means that you should never put anything underneath the head!

Then you can call the emergency squad. If not for yourself, then do it for the attacker. Why? Because you only wanted to stop his attack and didn't want to kill him on purpose, or did you? In a later court case this can be an important aspect.

2.4.5. CONTACT WITH POLICE

The police will come soon. Don't run toward the officer, full of joy and with your weapon in hand, in order to fling your arms around his or her neck. Stay calm (easier said than done) and polite. Indicate that

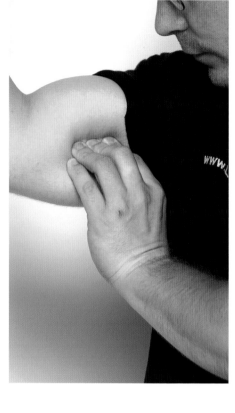

Compression of the leg's artery while lying down. Here you have to use a lot of pressure for the compression of the artery in the groin against the thighbone. This is very difficult to do alone.

Compression of the upper arm, with injuries below this point. The artery runs between both muscles of the upper arm (biceps and triceps) and can be pressed against the bone.

you have been attacked, feared for your life, and had to defend yourself. Point out that you have a weapon and—very important—ask what is now expected of you.

Expect that your "saviors" at least have their hands touching their pistol or are even pointing it at you. Don't take this personally; this is a question of self-protection. The officers will advise you to put down your weapon, and you will surely be searched and perhaps handcuffed.

Don't struggle, and wait until you are able to tell your story. For the police the image looks like this: you are standing—totally distraught—with the knife in your hands while somebody is lying on the ground, bleeding. Think about how this would look to you.

When you are then asked to give your statement, you ought to signal your willingness to cooperate clearly and politely, but ask for a transport to the hospital because of your condition. Assure the officers that you will then be at their disposal, together with your lawyer. This way you make sure that you are medically okay, and in addition you have the chance to get back to your senses a bit more. You don't have to make any statements that would incriminate yourself. By the time you have to testify again, it is hoped that all witnesses will have made clear who really was the aggressor.

2.4.6. WHY EVERYTHING?

I believe that self-defense is more than the actual physical component. I don't defend just my life or my physical integrity. I also defend my lifestyle: my freedom to go wherever I want to go, to play sports, and to meet my friends.

Macho sayings that—especially on the internet—make it clear to everyone that the writer of this wisdom would rather be in court for homicide than bow to insult are childish and stupid.

In this book we concretely talk about using weapons for defense. Responsibility and accepting the rules of society belong to this. I am not in favor of taking a risk, but I am for behaving in accordance with the law. An armed argument will be followed up by official investigation and perhaps a court case. Thus, it should be in your own interest to optimize your self-defense with respect to surviving on the streets as well as in court.

Shock position, using a bag
underneath the legs

CHAPTER THREE
SELF-DEFENSE WITH TOOLS

The market of tools for self-defense is gigantic. Entire branches of industry do research and produce in this area. As always, economic interests are involved. Consequently, the promises and statements about the potential of these tools are flamboyant. But, of course, no all-in-one device exists that is suitable for all purposes. The question is what a tool for defense is supposed to do, and what the requirements are for such a tool.

3.1. THE EFFECT

If you deal with this topic scientifically, you will find that most research is about the "man-stopping" effect of weapons. This denomination initially stems from the realm of firearms but still has significance for other tools and self-defense devices, but in a slightly modified form. Much is debated about the abilities and inabilities of weapons. But ultimately there is only one concrete criterion for judging the effectiveness of a tool in accordance with our defense-oriented viewpoint. This criterion is its stopping ability.

To begin with, it is totally unimportant how a weapon works, which reactions it will evoke in the attacker, how easily it can be used, or what its later effects are. These criteria are only of secondary importance and have to be looked at with respect to the weapon's use. But first of all it is imperative that the weapon or tool fulfills its intended function. Ideally, the

use of the weapon should stop the attack immediately and at once. Here, "at once" means in the same fraction of a second that the weapon is deployed, not a second later or even minutes later.

And this is exactly the problem with almost all weapons. Hollywood and the internet have contributed to the rule of only vague knowledge with respect to stopping effects—even in the professional area. Distinctly too much potential, for example, is always attributed to firearms. Weapons are also judged under laboratory conditions, which don't have anything to do with actual use.

No portable weapon can immediately stop an attack the moment it is used. By "immediately," I mean just that. But the attacker may die after finishing his or her attack. This is a situation that often can occur when using firearms against a knife attack. The attacker mortally wounds the person carrying a firearm, although the attacker himself or herself is already hit in the chest by bullets. Nothing is won in this case, neither the life of the defender nor that of the attacker.

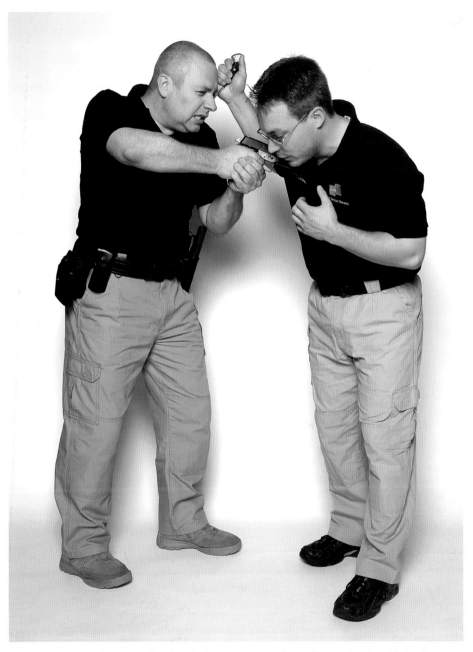

At short distances below 23 feet (7 m), the person carrying a firearm is often hit by the blade despite shooting.

3.2. FIREARMS AGAINST ATTACKERS WITH KNIVES

In 1983, the American *SWAT Magazine* published an article by Dennis Tueller with the title "How Close Is Close?" Sgt. Tueller, of the Salt Lake City, Utah, police department, had realized that there were ambiguities within the police community with respect to the concepts of fighting off knife attacks. The foremost question was how far away an attacker with an edged weapon has to be from an officer in order for the officer to have enough time to draw the firearm and stop the attacker with gunshots before being hit himself or herself.

The tests conducted by Tueller were simple: he measured the time an officer needed for drawing the weapon and shooting at a target at a distance of 21 feet (6.5 m). Times of about 1.5 seconds were typical. Especially well-trained officers had times a bit below that (about 1.3 to 1.4 seconds).

Tueller then posed the question of how long an attacker takes to cover this distance of about 21 feet (6.5 m). He came to the result that this, too, takes about 1.5 seconds.

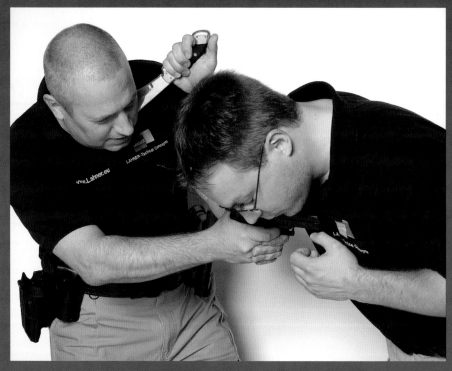

The attacker (right) falls into the defender (left, with pistol) due to the attack's momentum and severely injures him in the area of the chest/neck.

This fact clearly resulted in the following conclusion: every attacker armed with a blade poses a deadly threat for somebody carrying a firearm within a radius of at least 21 feet. Even if the person carrying a firearm is able to shoot, this will influence the attacker only after contact, which means the weapon bearer is already injured. In reality, you have to count on the situation being even more complicated. First you have to detect the attacker, then assess the actual danger. Furthermore, you have to add various factors of the surroundings, such as possibilities for evasion, spatial situation, clothing, holster, weapon type, and others. The most difficult thing is the shoot/no-shoot decision, which means an unequivocal identification of the situation as a justification for using the firearm. Even if you put aside all these problems of reality and create a "quasi laboratory situation," there are still great difficulties for the user of firearms. First of all, it has to be clear that the shooter has to move. Over short distances the importance of moving increases. While across a distance of 23 feet (7 m) a lateral movement may be sufficient to let the attacker hit empty space, this is not possible for distances below 13 feet (4 m). And classic firearm training doesn't incorporate movements sufficiently.

This is because the majority of all attacks occur by surprise, and for police officers during routine situations, the actual distances are smaller by far. Here another kind of defense besides shooting has to be used. How exactly this can look would lead us too far afield here. But nevertheless I want to talk about some of the problematic items at this point: the classic two-handed grip usually takes too much time and also requires a too-static position. And here, one or two steps are also "static." An often-offered solution is protection by a kind of blocking or protective movement against the knife attack by using the free hand, while firing at the same time.

But this results in many risks, an important element of which is that an edged weapon cannot be simply blocked. Neither can it be avoided that the blade reaches the defender across the block, nor is contact with the arm harmless.

Especially the second case quite often is not obvious. But let's assume the defender at first can stop the attack with his or her arm. What happens if the attacker injures the arm? Many people think here that the arm can be sacrificed. Well, it is not that simple. If your arm is cut, you instinctively pull it back, even without consciously feeling the pain.

This natural protection from injury even happens when you cut yourself on paper in the office. If you pay close attention, you will realize that the movement happens first, and only afterward do you feel the pain. This rebuts the statement that you don't feel the pain while under stress.

The arm moves and thus exposes the area to be protected, usually the neck and head. This way the target is immediately accessible for a second attack, leading to mortal injuries. Most attacks consist of rapid, successive cuts or stabs. Even if you can fire a bullet after the first attack and successfully stop it, there is enough time for further and fatal hits.

Thus you can see: defense against knife attacks is not as easy as is frequently stated. Not even for people carrying firearms. But solutions exist, one of which is based on using the firearm for stopping, deflecting, and controlling the blade. Imagine that a blade is racing toward you. Would you rather hold up your arm against it or your weapon? The weapon at least is made of steel and plastics insensitive to pain and extremely hard. Shooting doesn't help you any way because of the close distance.

These concepts can be practiced easily. But, to use a term commonly heard in English-speaking countries, a "reality check" is definitely recommended for whoever thinks that he or she will be able to defend themselves against perilous threats with minimal training.

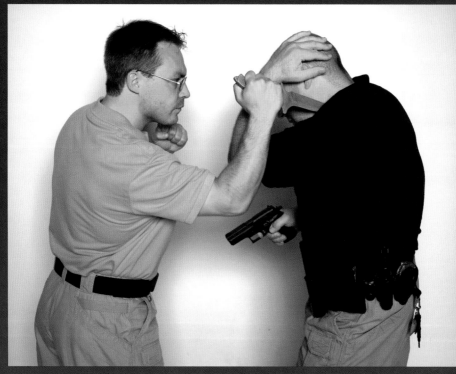

Despite the defender's block, the blade reaches up to the neck. The attacking arm is stopped, but the blade isn't stopped early enough. Using the firearm only is not sufficient at this distance.

While drawing the firearm, the defender is too close to the attacker *(at right)*.

The defender hits the firearm forcefully against the attacking weapon arm.

The defender *(at left)* hits against the weapon arm and practically stops it. The other arm serves as additional safety.

The firearm stays down so as not to hit yourself (for example, when trying a shot in the head); the arms open up.

The first shot hits the hip. Then follow-up shots are fired in a line extending upward (zipper) until the attack ends. By doing this, distance is created.

3.3. WEAPONS FOR SELF-DEFENSE

Weapons can be split into different categories, each with typical qualities and problems. I'll briefly introduce some of these categories, but only as an overview.

3.3.1 IMPACT TOOLS

Impact tools are weapons for hitting. A typical type of impact tool is an expandable baton or the tonfa, but also the palm stick and kubotan. By hitting, they transfer energy onto the attacker and in this way can cause pain and injuries. Their effect depends on how sensitive the attacker is to pain and whether a hit will also destroy bones or joints, thus impeding their function. Of course, the defender has to be within reach of the opponent.

3.3.2. FIREARMS

Firearms, for most people, have a rather subordinate relevance. Within the distances they are most commonly used at, they fulfill their task with respect to the immediate stopping effect much worse than is often believed. Quite often, firearms are used at distances that are considerably too short. Thus they can't play out their potential.

The defender doesn't have to be within contact range of the attacker; a firearm is even of clear advantage if he or she is far away. But in real situations the attacker is usually way too close. Only new concepts of using a firearm in close proximity (e.g., "Extreme Close-Quarter Shooting") can deal with this complex of problems. Government agencies and the military are increasingly interested in methods in this field.

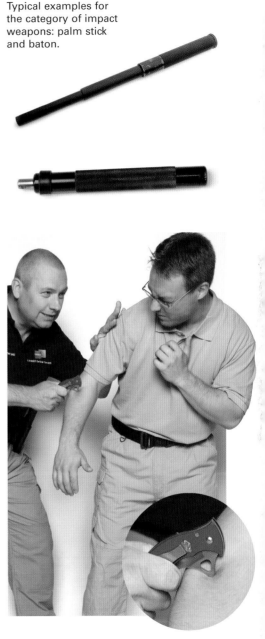

Typical examples for the category of impact weapons: palm stick and baton.

The Close Range Medium Impact Tool (CRMIPT), a noncutting tool by Bram Frank that is based on the functionality of a knife. Even hits and pressure on an arm are painful and effective. "Hammering" with the CRMIPT can lead to success in many situations.

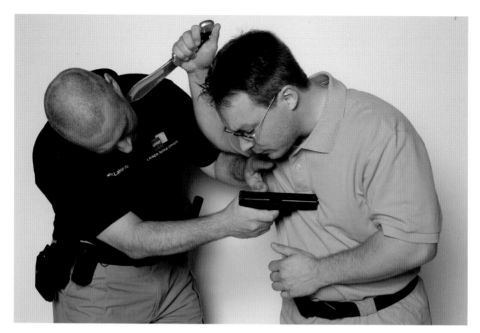

Who has an advantage here? Probably no one. Such problematic situations often occur when firearms and blades encounter each other at realistic distances.

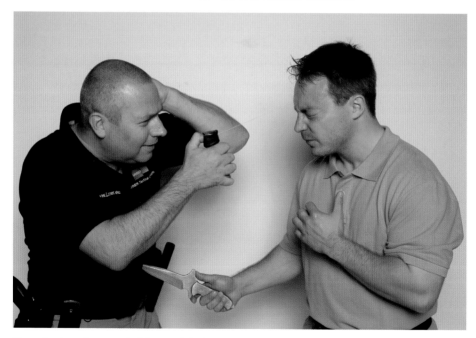

Here, the impairment of vision and the impact of the OC spray are well visible. But you can also see that the knife attack isn't stopped by this.

3.3.3. CHEMICAL WEAPONS

Chemical weapons (e.g., CS, OC, CN) can be used as a means for enforcement or for opening possible escape ways. They can hardly stop an attack in the literal sense. In particular, OC spray, also called pepper spray, has to be viewed critically. On the one hand, OC spray is not permitted for use against humans in Germany, but on the other hand, OC is not a miraculous silver bullet. An attack already taking place that is led with impetus and intent can't be stopped by OC. Or the effects of the spray occur with the attacker only after the defender has already been hit. Surely some sprays are helpful weapons in defense, but under no circumstances should they be overrated.

3.3.4. ELECTRIC WEAPONS

Stun guns are supposed to render the attacker unable to fight, by means of electric discharges. While in theory they should fulfill the criterion of immediate stopping, in practice this is rarely the case. Type of clothing, individual pain threshold, and placement of a hit limit their usefulness. More-powerful variants, such as the Tasers used in the United States, on the one hand are not allowed in Germany according to the German weapons law, and on the other hand, they are limited by the number of shots. They are increasingly critically questioned with respect to their role as "less lethal" or "nonlethal" tools. And here, too, sufficient examples exist for their nonimmediate stopping effect. Thus, they may be expedient for government agencies but are not suitable for use against normal life-threatening attacks.

3.3.5. EDGED WEAPONS

If you don't fall for Hollywood myths or stories about "the knifer" but are ready to objectively deal with knives for self-defense, the following becomes obvious: at close range, edged weapons have the highest potential with respect to the stopping effect. In contrast to impact tools and chemical means, blades can stop an attack immediately.

BUT: they can do so only with the right training and the right technique of use! The line between criminal behavior and legitimate self-defense is thin. And only the training with a tool (irrespective of its type) gives you the capability to survive the confrontation (as well as the legal aftermath, when it comes to it).

Knives and cutting tools offer many advantages. First, blades don't need any force. A good knife is sharp and cuts all by itself along its edge. Therefore the success of an act of defense is mostly independent of factors such as body size, weight, and force. Thus, blades become the ideal tool for weaker humans, senior citizens, or women.

Contact with the blade alone can already result in serious injuries. Disarming or wresting the knife away is as good as impossible. Although this is often trained, and neck-breaking techniques can be seen during training, an attacker with a knife can't be disarmed with one's bare hands. This technique ought to be practiced nevertheless, but only to realize a position for disarming, in case you can attain such a position by chance and with a lot of luck.

By the way, the same is valid for the confrontation of knife versus stick. You can knock a knife out of the hands only of a harmless "poser." An attack led with intent lets all assumed advantages of reach vanish like smoke. Even if you hit the person carrying a knife, you usually just exchange a hit for a stab or cut.

Edged weapons don't have a great deal of these problems. In this book you will see that cutting is better for our purposes than stabbing, because our intention is to stop the attack. Stabs are less able to do that than cuts and are also more lethal.

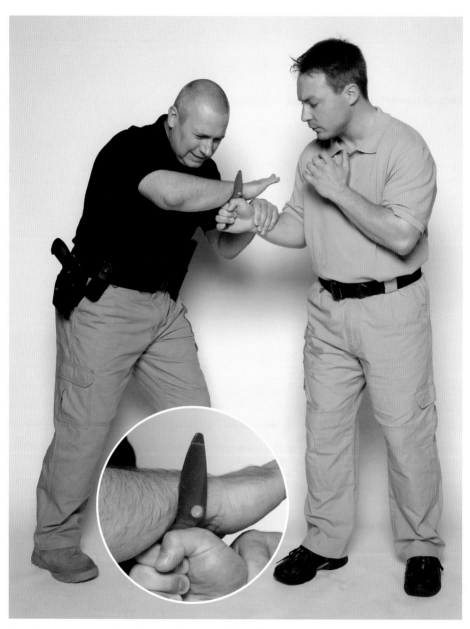

A typical attempt at disarming as it is trained in self-defense systems: it may work where it originates—fending off big machetes—but not with a typical folder, as shown here.

In the inset you can see the cut into the defender's disarming arm as a result of the knife's small size and the lack of control over the attacker's thumb.

Injuries like this can easily penetrate down to the bone and impair the hand's function. Here, an injury of the artery is likely too.

The knife attacker sacrifices his arm, which is likely to be broken. By doing this, he gets the opportunity to initiate a potentially lethal attack toward the belly.

The impact of the stick on the arm is painful and leads to injuries but is not lethal.

CHAPTER FOUR
CHOICE OF A SUITABLE KNIFE

The interaction of tool and concept of usage is important for a successful defense. I will introduce these concepts in the following chapters, but here I want to go into detail with respect to choosing a suitable tool.

An old adage in the world of firearms is "Better a small pocket revolver at hand than a large-caliber gun in the safe at home." Only the tool you have with you in an emergency is able to help. Thus, decide on a knife size you are willing to carry around almost all the time.

I call this "the umbrella method." As you know, if you leave home without an umbrella, it will surely rain, but if you have an umbrella with you, this is only rarely the case.

Via the size of the knife, we immediately come to its construction type. Fixed blades (here, handle and blade form a stable unit) are very stable and almost indestructible. They are also less problematic in stressful situations because they

neither require a complicated drawing procedure nor fine motor skills for opening. On the other hand, fixed blades are larger than folding knives ("folders") of the same blade length, due to their construction type.

Böker Plus MA-2

Böker Plus Subcom
Fixed Blade

Cherusker Magnum LLC

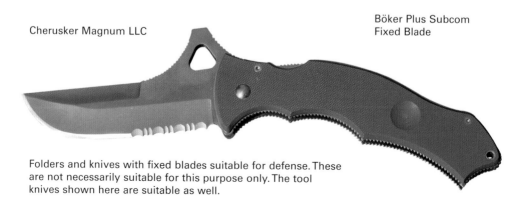

Folders and knives with fixed blades suitable for defense. These are not necessarily suitable for this purpose only. The tool knives shown here are suitable as well.

For a folder, there always has to be an opening process before the tool is ready for use. This is not free of problems, because it requires certain fine motor skills that quickly dwindle under stress. Furthermore, opening the knife is always an additional step that has to be done in the chain of actions for defense measures. Few knives on the market offer solutions with respect to this point. The best one, in my opinion, is Bram Frank's "kinetic opening": here, the knife is opened directly at the attacker's body. This is done by means of a coarse motor process, which, in addition, doesn't have to be integrated into the defense as a separate step. The first hit opens the knife, if necessary.

Fixed blades don't have to be unfolded, but they have other problems, because in everyday life, not every contemporary is enthusiastic and appreciative if he or she realizes you are carrying a knife. But if a fixed blade has to be carried unobtrusively, quite often its handle is less ergonomic and too small. Everybody has to choose for themselves which factors predominate. By now a number of fixed blades are available that are small but nevertheless can be handled comfortably.

Because I am, of course, convinced of the high quality of my own work, I want to recommend the Wa2Go (see page 15) to you. The "Way to Go" is a pure utility knife. It was designed following the principles of Bram Frank, all of which I believe to be very reasonable. The goal in developing the Wa2Go was to find an alternative to single-handed folding knives, which are usually meant less as weapons but are very good working tools.

The Wa2Go fills this gap because the handle is large enough to securely hold it and use it for heavy work. On the other hand, it is small enough to carry with

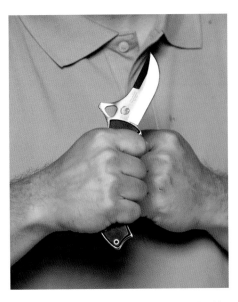

The Cherusker knife Lapu Lapu Corto (LLC) is a Bram Frank design. It has an outstanding handle suitable for reliable handling and with more than just sufficient stability.

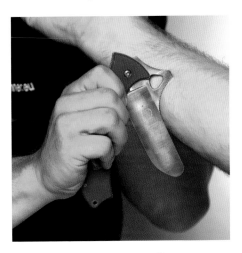

A hit onto an arbitrary target (here, an arm as example) leads to the blade's opening by means of a ramp. This example is an exercise and is not representative of a realistic situation. You can clearly see how the ramp catches at the arm and then turns the moveable blade via the axis. The handle is reliable and stable, even under stress, because of its good handle design.

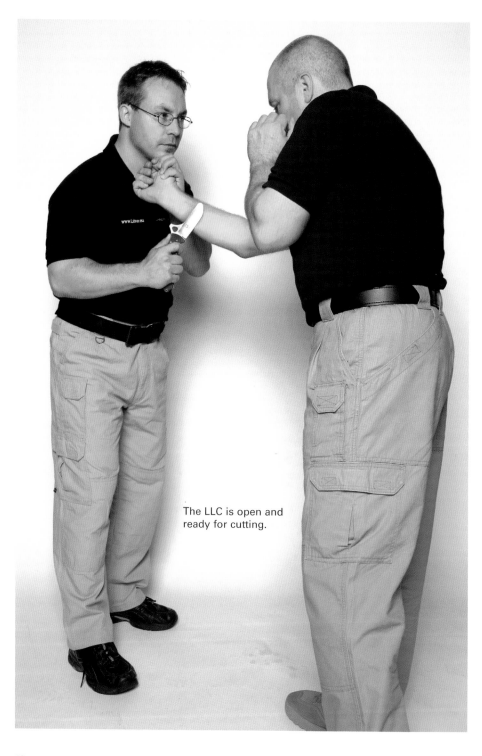

The LLC is open and ready for cutting.

you all the time. It is not a fighting knife, because it lacks essential attributes such as warding and deflecting elements. But every good utility knife can be used for self-defense, because a good knife is characterized by a comfortable handle, good balance, and ergonomics. No more and no less.

4.1. THE HANDLE

The most important part of a knife is—did you guess it right?—the handle. The blade length, in comparison, is less important. Of what use is the longest blade if you can hold the knife only between two fingers, or if there is the danger that your hand slips into the blade edge?

A good handle fits your hand size. A piece of steel protruding from the handle can also be used for hitting, levering, or latching onto something, in case less drastic techniques than cutting can also lead to the goal. A folder, for example, can also be used in closed position in case cutting is not justified or necessary. Bram Frank's knives are especially constructed for this case. This is a factor that should also be met, within limits, by the knife of your choice. At least it should be possible to apply pressure or execute a hit with the closed knife.

While under stress, you should also not lose control over the knife with wet, bloody, or sweaty hands. This is ensured by the use of nonslip materials such as G-10 or micarta, but also by a lot of other materials. Many handles have ergonomic disadvantages. For example, their cross section may be too round, and thus instinctive orientation is not possible: you don't automatically know where the blade edge is without looking at the knife.

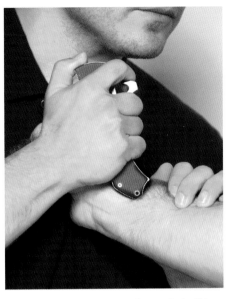

Here, the attacker's access is warded off by a hit or painful pressure of the knife's handle butt on the arm. The handle's shape allows for various grips and use as a weapon. Opening the blade here is neither proportionate nor necessary.

Cherusker knife by Bram Frank. The color coding, as with firearms, allows reliable identification (red = training knife, blue = noncutting tool, black = sharp knife).

I have heard many complaints from the military. Many soldiers report that they couldn't tell in the dark (all the more while wearing gloves) whether the blade edge was facing toward the front, the back, or sideways—a potentially fatal situation. When choosing a knife, take into account that you are hardly able to deal with compromises in handling the knife under stress.

The handle's shape also adds to your safety; it ought to prevent your hand from sliding onto the blade edge. This can be achieved by a swell or a guard toward the blade or, even better, by well-fitting finger grooves. With these you may even be able to choose the position of your grip (either more toward the handle's end or more in the direction of the blade), and you are even able to control the knife if your grip is rather slack. Test different models of the knives you are considering for purchase. Among knives that otherwise have the same qualities, choose the one whose handle has the most natural feel for you.

4.2. THE BLADE SHAPE

There are a lot of discussions about the blade shape, and right now the market is almost chock-full of the most-adventurous shapes. Here it is essential: the blade shape depends only on what you intend to do with the tool. For our purposes we search for a blade that is especially well suited for cutting because—as you will see later—my concepts in self-defense with the knife especially emphasize cutting. Thus the blade of your knife should be a bit curved, since a curved blade with short dimensions has a rather long cutting edge. This results in a knife that is not disruptive in daily routine and also has quite good cutting abilities.

At least as many discussions exist about whether the blade edge should be smooth or serrated or both. The supporters of serrated blades argue that with a short blade you have a considerably higher cutting performance. And, indeed, mate-

A blade that is curved rather than straight provides a long edge despite having a rather short blade length.

Blades can be either smooth (plain) or have teeth (serrated) or exhibit either along different blade sections.

rials such as ropes and cardboard can be severed easier with a serrated edge. On the other hand, serrated blades catch onto clothing more easily. Under stress, chances are high that you will lose the knife.

Advocates of simple, smooth blades don't know this problem. However, the cutting performance is a bit weaker. Since a knife for self-defense should be especially sharp, smooth blades without serrations have the advantage that they can easily be resharpened manually. But ultimately this discussion is rather academic; I couldn't find any serious differences during cutting tests.

A very good compromise, and the best of both worlds, is the semiserrated blade. Here, too, the serrated parts are not as easy to resharpen as the smooth parts. But there is no argument against carrying a second, small tool knife (Swiss army knife) along. This way you also have a screwdriver, nail file, and corkscrew with you and are best suited for all the "challenges of everyday life."

I don't want to start discussions about the steel type here. Ultimately, the only requirement I have for a knife is that it be sharp, stay sharp for a long period of time (if possible), and at the same time be easy to resharpen. In particular, the last point is a bit problematic with modern high-performance steels.

4.3. CLIP AND HOLSTER

Your defense knife is not of much use if it is buried deep inside your trouser pocket. Only if you are able to draw the knife quickly do you have a certain chance to defend yourself. Almost all modern folders have a so-called clip, which allows you to secure the knife firmly in the pocket and to always have it at hand in an emergency.

It should be possible to retrofit the clip from one side to the other in order to be able to carry the knife on the right side as

A typical folder with clip for secure carrying in one's trouser pocket

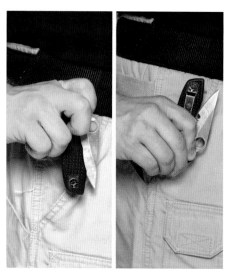

Tip-down carry: the tip points downward and the access is at the axis.

Tip-up carry: the blade's tip points upward and you grip the handle at its rear end when drawing the folder.

well as the left side. Depending on where the clip is located in relation to the knife's tip, it is called either "tip up" or "tip down" carrying. If the knife tip shows upward, potentially—if you have bad luck—you might grab the blade tip in the event that the blade has moved outside the handle due to heavy percussion or vibration. But in the end, tip up versus tip down is a matter of taste. Just test what you prefer.

The best possibilities for drawing a knife quickly in case of an attack are offered by a holster. In earlier times they were often made of leather, but nowadays they are made of thermoplastics such as Kydex. These holsters are adjusted optimally to the surface and shape of the knife, while at the same time holding it securely and easily accessible at the belt. Of course, the holster is slightly visible underneath your clothing. But, in my opinion, this disadvantage is more than balanced by the advantage in speed when drawing the knife.

This is true anyway for fixed blades. It is important to find a knife with a sheath suitable for everyday routine. Here, too, modern plastics such as Kydex are available that impose practically no limits on the design of the sheath. Thus, a small knife with a fixed blade can be used well in everyday life and is easily accessible.

A fixed blade is less obtrusive if you choose the method of carrying called IWB (inside waistband). Here, the knife is put inside the waistband by means of a special flat sheath and is secured at the belt with a band or cord. This way only the handle can be seen, which rests very close to the body. The disadvantage of this way of carrying is the danger of hurting yourself when putting the knife into the sheath. Accordingly, the sheath should be pulled out of the trousers when putting the knife back into its sheath. But more important for defense

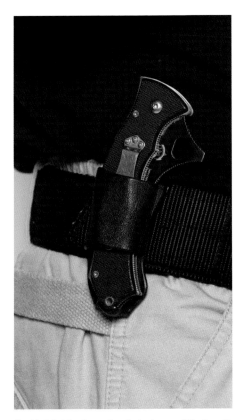

An LLC folder in a simple holster of Kydex. It doesn't stick out, and the process of drawing is quick despite the knife's firm attachment.

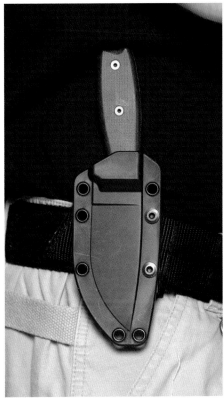

A fixed-blade Ontario RAT3 with Kydex sheath

is the ability to quickly draw the knife. You have to choose the way of carrying in accordance with the usage, the situation, your body characteristics, and your clothing.

A favorite topic, especially among collectors, is this: How many knives do you need? Ultimately, it is better to get acquainted with handling a single knife than changing your knife daily and not being able to handle it in an emergency. Get used to a knife that you carry all the time and that you use in training. Nevertheless, it is worth a thought to carry a second, small knife on the nondominant side of your body. This may be the tool for everyday work that we were talking about before. In case of an injury to your dominant hand or in case you lose your knife, it can serve as a backup solution.

But count on the fact that some of your contemporaries will look with distrust at you wearing two knives or even one. You should be especially wary in case of identity checks by police officers. In case your knives are visible when you reach for your papers, inform the police officers prior to moving that you have two knives with you, and ask for exact instructions.

4.4. THE PROCESS OF DRAWING THE KNIFE

Regardless of holster, clip, sheath, or another type of carrying system, concealed carry, which is advisable for avoiding unnecessary attention, is the biggest hurdle in the drawing process because it costs additional time. Therefore you ought to sufficiently train in drawing the knife from concealed-carry positions. And, of course, you should not do so only when wearing a training outfit, but also while wearing the clothing you wear in everyday life.

**Wearing under Clothing
Closed at the Front**

Your free hand grabs the fabric of your clothing at the chest, then moves upward for blocking. This way you bring that hand into a defined position and make way for your weapon hand to grasp the knife. The process of drawing follows.

In a second variant, the free hand goes up to the chest, and the weapon hand with outstretched thumb pushes the clothing out of the way. But this requires a relatively loose fit of your clothing and good control

Starting position with closed jacket

The free hand grabs the seam of the jacket; the weapon hand starts its downward path from cover.

While the left hand pulls the jacket upward, the weapon hand can help, if necessary.

The free hand is on the chest and holds the jacket; the weapon hand encloses the knife handle fully and firmly.

The drawing process starts with a direct path vertically upward.

The knife has been drawn and protects the upper torso. Now the free hand can let go of the jacket and is also available for defense.

over your jacket. The knife's handle should not tend to hang on the clothing, and heavy jackets cannot be moved this way either. But this allows your second hand to always be available for blocking and covering or to control the opponent for a short time during a confrontation.

Wearing under Clothing
Open at the Front

In principle, you can act likewise with clothing open at the front. In an interesting variation, the free hand pulls on the left jacket side toward the front and body center, thus uncovering the knife on the right side.

The free hand provides protection in the upper area. The weapon hand's thumb is pointing upward, such as with a hitchhiker, and pushes underneath the jacket.

The thumb pushes the jacket upward until the knife handle is accessible for the same hand.

Then the knife can be grabbed and the movement upward can be started.

End position after the drawing process

Train these procedures time and again. Your tool is not very helpful if you can't draw it quickly enough in an emergency. Especially with different dress styles, you may be required to be proficient in various carry methods and drawing processes. For folders the drawing process follows the same principles.

Defensive posture with open jacket

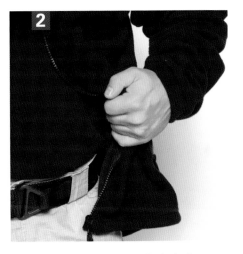

Access with the left hand at the jacket's seam, and starting of the pull toward the left ear

By pulling the jacket on the left, the knife on the right becomes accessible. The left hand has reached a position for cover.

Now, grabbing the knife has become possible.

The knife has been drawn; a defensive posture has been taken. The left hand can now be freely used.

CHAPTER FIVE
KNIVES FOR TRAINING

When training for defense with a knife, you need to have a training knife. One or, better, several are worth their weight in gold, because by means of these nondangerous utilities you develop all the necessary capabilities for defending yourself in an emergency. Many people forget about this and acquire one expensive knife after another. But if your interest is in using knives and not just collecting them, then you'd better invest a bit of money in a good knife for training.

Don't forget this important basic principle: "All knives are sharp!" Never

Training with sharp blades excludes real contact. Here you can clearly see that a safety distance of at least 12 to 20 inches (30–50 cm) has to be chosen. Of course, you will get used to a wrong feeling of distance and timing. Nevertheless, this is still dangerous.

train—and I really do mean "never"—with a sharp knife. Treat all your knives, even your training knives, as if they were sharp. This way you don't get used to any bad habits that could be your downfall with sharp knives. Taping the blade, which is practiced time and again, is also a gross negligence that sooner or later will cost you dearly in training.

An essential aspect of training with weapons is to get a feel for the reach, timing, and contact with the weapon. A training knife allows you to really defend against a knife attack with your weapon and to make counterattacks while, with your blade, keeping in steady contact with the opponent.

Many people think that training with sharp weapons is indispensable for dealing with the dangers of a blade. But actually you only practice wrong timing and wrong distance by doing so—and mistakes in training will have severe consequences in real-life situations. It is better if you analyze exactly what you are doing, and be honest toward yourself. With training knives, too, you can determine exactly when you got cut or when you didn't reach your opponent.

Unfortunately, the market for training knives is very meager. The rubber knives available everywhere are too flexible to do the job properly. Rubber also impedes the movements of the knife on the skin of your opponent, and, after an hour of training, your partner will complain bitterly about you. Wooden knives are usually too pointed, may splinter dangerously, and are deficient with respect to their shape. Most times you can't see exactly where the blade starts and ends. In addition, the round handle impedes orientation of the blade.

Typical wooden and rubber knives are suitable for training only within certain limits.

The sharp knife and the version for training are equal up to small details.

Your best bet is to train with a training knife similar in size and shape to the original knife you carry with you. Only in this way can you develop a feel for the characteristics of your knife, judge the reach of your knife correctly, and know about the peculiarities of your special model.

For a few knives on the market, there are already training knives available that are identical in construction and differ from the original only in their blunt blade. If you carry a knife for which such a training version is available, this is optimal, of course. In case you choose another knife, you should look for training models.

These versions should belong to your collection of knives for training:

plastic trainer: This should be identical in construction to the original. For folders, this is ideally a set with an open and a closed version. With these you can work with your partner by using medium contact. You will get a feel for impinging the blade and cutting with it. In addition, the trainer really stops the attack and doesn't bend.

soft trainer: This training knife is meant for hard contact and is suitable for rapid scenarios, with only little danger of injuries. On the other hand, it is not very stable, and an attack can't always be stopped because the material gives way.

marking knife: Especially in rapid sequences, quite often you are unable to follow who was cut where. During training you are often convinced that you didn't even get a single scratch. A marking knife leaves its incorruptible color trace. But the most important job of this training utility is to ensure that you don't cut yourself. This is the case more often than you might think.

metal trainer: Metal gives you a realistic feel for the material and its weight. But it allows only slow and very careful training. I believe that this tool rather than anything else is expendable.

Plastic trainer for
riskless training

Soft trainer for
harder contact

Trainer made
of metal

Marking knife
for sparring
with feedback

CHAPTER SIX

BIOMECHANICAL CUTTING

You have seen me talking about a "tool" time and again instead of using the word "knife." This is because I want to avoid emphasizing the means of its use too much. Sure, a good knife is important, and we already know a couple of criteria for such a knife. On the other hand, it is useless or even dangerous to have the newest and most dangerous "tactical high-gloss quick-kill folder" with you, decorated with macho proverbs, without having any training experience. Here, any knife cult is out of place.

By means of the proper training, all aspects of use turn into utilities for defense. You should never underestimate the user and his or her system. The tool in your hand is able to optimize only what the user has to offer with respect to proficiency and concepts.

This way we arrive at the concepts of using the knife as a tool for self-defense. We now know that the decisive factor is the so-called stopping effect of the tool that is used. Knives have a very high stopping effect, which even surpasses that of firearms at distances between 0 and 16.4 feet (0–5 m). But this can be guaranteed only if the knife is used with the proper concepts.

In the use of knives you especially have to distinguish between cutting and stabbing techniques. First we want to look at the stabbing techniques: stabs are made with the blade tip and penetrate the attacker's body. There they create a wound channel that is about as deep as the blade is long, and sometimes a bit longer due to compression. On the way into the tissue, the blade tip first displaces material that then is severed by the blade edge. In contrast to firearms, the created wound channel of the blade is similar to the blade's dimensions

The adverse effect on the attacker is due mostly to the injury of vital organs and blood vessels and the resulting shock from the amount of lost blood. All other statements, such as about the famous nervous shock due to stabbing the kidney, often taught for "taking out sentries" in the military, have to be treated with great caution.

Stabs accordingly have some serious disadvantages: on the one hand, stabs in most cases are life threatening or even lethal, and on the other hand, the stopping effect is based on the attacker's bleeding to death or being shocked. Depending on where the hit is placed, this can take between a few seconds and several minutes. Regarding the length of time for this to occur, all the experts in the field usually quarrel. Free from any anatomical knowledge and even less enlightened by physiology or pathology, the craziest discussions unfold.

But in this age of video surveillance, it is surprising to see real confrontations, some of which involve dozens of stabs to the upper torso and belly. Even more, when the culprit has run off, in some cases you can see the victim still staggering around for half a minute before he or she finally collapses.

The time that passes until the opponent is completely unable to fight can be copiously used to attack you. Stabs are thus an extremely unreliable method for stopping and, in addition, end lethally in most cases.

Michael Janich, an excellent American trainer, has cowritten an interesting book with Christopher Grosz. In *Contemporary Knife Targeting*, he analyzes and in particular disproves "Timetable of Death" by William Fairbairn, used for decades and quoted many times. But most teaching statements with respect to the topic of defense and knife fights are based on exactly this.

Totally different than stabs are cuts such as the ones described in our defense concept as "biomechanical cutting," which are based on the concept that the human body at the level of biomechanics is nothing more than a machine functioning with the help of motors, block and tackle, hydraulic pipes, cables, and a calculator. In the event that important parts of this machine are damaged, its function suffers. This is exactly the goal of biomechanical cutting. The principle is to destroy the form in order to impair the function.

A simple example is the cutting attack toward your neck, starting from the left at the outside, similar to receiving a slap in the face while the attacker is holding a knife in the hand. An attempt to block the knife with your own left arm or to counter inevitably leads to severe cutting injuries of the arm. In contrast to sports training, the opponent either carries out the cut toward the neck or he immediately pulls back the knife when contacting the arm and cuts over the arm.

It makes much more sense to bring your own knife into contact with the attacking forearm in order to first stop the attack. The cut at the inside of the attacker's forearm severs the so-called flexor. This muscle and the connecting sinews cause clenching of the fist and thus are responsible for holding the knife. If the muscles are severed, the attacker's fist opens and the knife falls to the ground, or the knife attack is at least weakened. Nobody states that this always works 100 percent. But it is much more probable to achieve a functional impairment this way than to achieve an immediate stop of the attack by means of stabs to the belly.

Another advantage of this method is that the attacker exposes himself or herself and thus gives the defender access to their weapon arm. This way, while the attacker is in reach, the essential targets on the defender's body are protected. At this

Mike Janich (US), next to Bram Frank, is one of the trainers propagating functional cuts with knives.

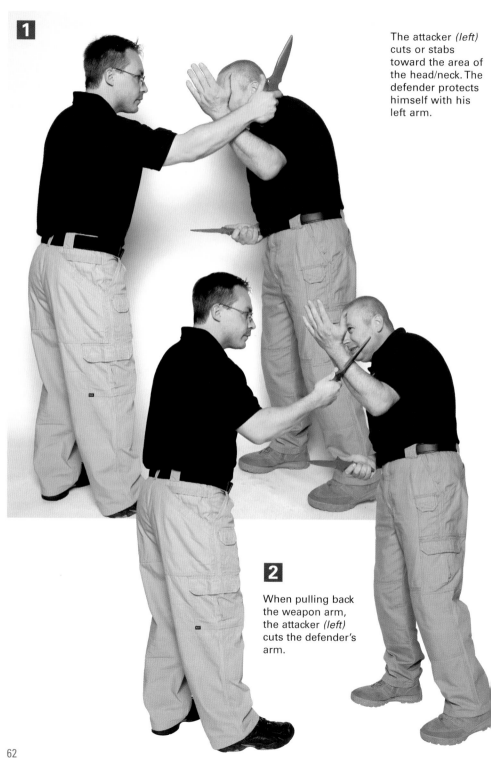

1

The attacker *(left)* cuts or stabs toward the area of the head/neck. The defender protects himself with his left arm.

2

When pulling back the weapon arm, the attacker *(left)* cuts the defender's arm.

3

The defender reflexively pulls back his arm and exposes his neck.

4

The attacker *(left)* is taking advantage and severely injures the defender. This cut has a very high potential of being lethal by injuring the neck's arteries.

point, conventional techniques quite often run into problems. To fend off a knife attack by means of stabs into the belly, chest, or neck results in the defender as well as the attacker being able to reach these vital targets. With biomechanical cutting, in contrast, the defender likely stays out of the attacker's reach, because he or she only has to reach up to the attacker's weapon arm.

At the same time, you can achieve an immediate stopping effect with biomechanical cutting. As opposed to attacks on the body, which take a long time until disablement of the opponent is achieved, here an immediate "biomechanical shutdown" is possible. This means that the attack is immediately stopped by means of the defender's blade. Some examples for better understanding: many muscle groups of the body are so-called antagonistic systems, which means that two or more muscles act against each other with their movements. The biceps, at the front of the upper arm, bends the arm at the elbow joint, while the triceps, at the back of the upper arm, stretches it. If one of these antagonistic muscles is damaged (e.g., severed), the function of the undamaged muscle dominates. In the same way, a cut

The attacker's arm *(right)* is stopped by the defender's blade *(left)*.

This way the lower arm's tendons relevant for gripping can be injured. There is no guarantee of this, but the reaction of the person being cut is usually very clear.

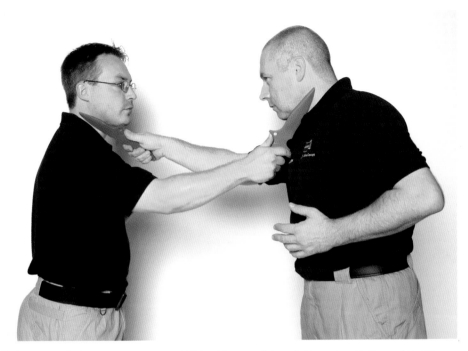

If the enemy is in range—so are you! This old proverb is valid here too. Both parties are within reach of the opponent's blade.

If the defender *(left)* forces the attacker to expose himself, the attacker's arm can be cut while vital targets of the defender are still out of reach.

at the thigh's front results in the leg bending, and a cut at the shoulder muscle prevents lifting the arm. Biomechanical cutting works independently of the attacker's emotional state, aggression, pain threshold, drug consumption, weight, force, and age.

Contrary to common opinion, a knife as "material splitter" is very effective at close range when you are knowledgable about some basic anatomical structures. Biomechanical cutting can be used very well in a fight under stress; in any case, it can be used as well or as badly as all the

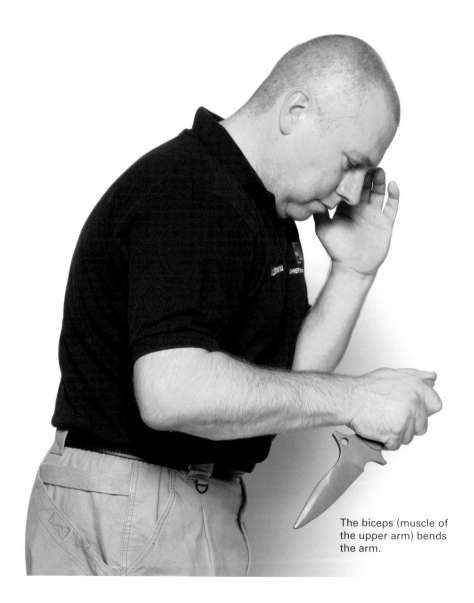

The biceps (muscle of the upper arm) bends the arm.

other techniques. But it is not a miraculous silver bullet, because you can't use it without previous training.

The idea of taking a weapon with you and using it in a fight without any training is naive. For any tool serving in defense, be it a flashlight or pepper spray, training is indispensable. Even and especially firearms, of which most people think that simply pulling the trigger is enough, require extensive training.

Many so-called experts caution against the use of tools and utilities for self-defense because they are presumed to be easy to

The triceps (muscle on the upper arm's backside) stretches the arm.

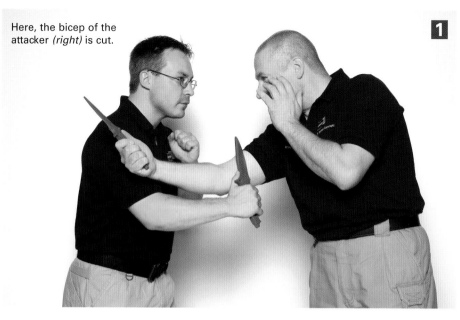

Here, the bicep of the attacker *(right)* is cut.

1

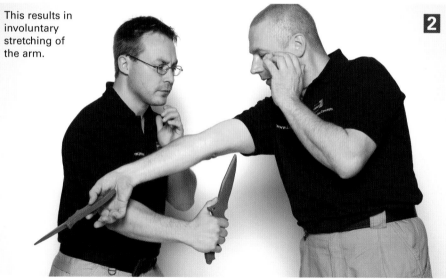

This results in involuntary stretching of the arm.

2

use against the defender himself or herself. To this I have to say that disarming, especially with knives, is a good deal more difficult than is commonly stated. Bram Frank likes to use the pictorial comparison with a kitchen appliance or shredder, and

he asks who would volunteer to reach toward the rotating parts in order to take out the blades. I don't want to add anything to this.

Biomechanical cutting thus has the great advantage that its stopping effect is

The following attempt to break the attacker's arm can't be counteracted.

very high. So tactically the best way to stop an attack is by means of cuts with a knife, not by stabbing, because with this technique the weapon arm of the attacker, but not of the defender, is always within reach. At the same time, this is a relatively safe method.

With respect to the inevitable legal aftermath of an armed confrontation, biomechanical cutting has an additional advantage: the intention of stopping but not killing an attacker is clearly emphasized. Naturally, here we assume a potentially lethal attack. At the same time our answer to it stays, in principle, below this level of escalation.

Of course, nobody will require us to take an unnecessarily high risk to fend off the attack. Here, I want to make clear once again that physical conflicts always bear the risk of severe injuries or even death. But in case conflict can't be avoided, biomechanical cutting is the least dangerous possibility of defense, with the highest stopping effect.

Last but not least, biomechanical cutting also ensures a certain moral and ethical component. The defense is directed against the attacking extremity and not the person behind it. The goal is to stop the attacker. The attacker's death is not the aim. I wouldn't go as far as to save the attacker's life on the price of my own life, but I believe that it is not up to humans to decide about life and death. The bottom line is that biomechanical cutting is the best tactical, legally justifiable, and ethical option.

CHAPTER SEVEN
THE MODULAR SYSTEM

The Modular System by Bram Frank is an intelligent teaching and training concept that allows the users to learn to defend themselves against attacks in a very short time. Here, series of attacks and counter-attacks are trained in so-called modules. Each module contains three types of attack and the suitable defense and counter techniques. In addition, special attributes (such as timing, coordination, and defense principles) are taught.

These modules initially entail training with blade against blade because the use of the knife in a precise way teaches angle of attack, timing, coordination, steps, and patterns of movement. Here, the emphasis is not on detailed techniques but on motor concepts and principles that can be transferred to any other kind of weapon or bare hands. This way you don't have to change your concept of application with each change of weapons (weapon transition). In the professional area, quite often problems arise because a weapon transition also means a change in usage concepts. Under stress, this is possible only with extreme amounts of training, and even then it does not always guarantee success.

For civilians, the possibility of transferring concepts of application means that not only can the knife be used for self-defense, but also any other available items commonly used in everyday life (e.g., pen, umbrella, keys). At the same time, the level of escalation can be selected by the choice of tool. Using a ballpoint pen for

pain-inducing control of an attacker, for example, follows the same principles as techniques for stopping a knife.

7.1. STRESS AND GROSS MOTOR SKILLS

The movement of humans is controlled on various levels of complexity. The hierarchically constructed nervous system allows extremely fine movements. Folding origami as well as playing the guitar not only are high art but also are excellent examples of fine motor motion sequences.

What links playing the guitar to defense? Absolutely nothing. And this is exactly the problem with many systems that, with a lot of time and leisure, teach fine motor sequences for defense. Under stress, all the fine motor movement programs are lost. The higher the stress level, the more a human has to fall back on simple, basic, gross motor motion concepts. This way, fine motor programs first turn into complex motor and then gross motor programs.

This backward development comes with the loss of peripheral vision (tunnel vision), a rising heart rate, and the loss of the sense of time. All these are effects of the adrenaline release caused by stress. In this state, movements that require high dexterity or other fine motor qualities are no longer available. Movements become extremely coarse, uncoordinated, and excessive. If the stress rises even more, most people fall into so-called fetal conditions, which means lying on the ground in a rolled-up position with arms and legs tucked in.

But why is so much emphasis put on fine motor motion sequences in the martial arts? On the one hand—and this is totally legitimate—you always have to assume that the trained movements under stress are executed more sloppily than in a training situation. Thus it makes sense to keep a mental file on these movements, to a certain degree, in order to be able to access enough of them in an emergency. On the other hand, we have to admit that the martial arts in our times are mainly serving a meditative or sportive purpose. Even though many of these systems claim that self-defense is their priority, they mostly have a sporty or traditional character.

This is not really bad as long as you don't make the common error of believing that these techniques—in just the way they are trained—are suitable for defense. As a counterargument, contests or even fights with only a few rules often are mentioned where the athletes work with just these techniques. But the fact is that in these cases, highly trained athletes meet under controlled conditions (there are always rules!).

On television you can observe the training of these athletes in prefight reports while they perform the most-complicated technical combinations in a coordinated and elegant way. Strangely, these combinations can hardly be recognized during the later rounds of the fight, or they are totally replaced by a wild "hitting each other." Here, too, stress is the culprit.

Thus, when even highly trained martial artists are not capable of using the trained techniques under controlled con-

ditions, how the heck should you be able to do exactly this under mortal danger and fear for your life? Hence, it is recommended that you be able to draw from a pool of techniques that are essentially based on gross motor motion patterns. Such techniques can indeed be used for self-defense.

7.2. NATURAL AND TRAINED MOVEMENTS

In addition, a second problem complex shows up at this point: the discrepancy between natural and trained movements. Every human has a natural repertoire of protective and evasive movements. Under stress, these movements are instinctively used.

If you have practiced totally different protective movements over a longer period of time, a conflict arises with respect to the choice of the correct movement. The instinctive patterns compete with the trained ones. In the best-case scenario, a considerable delay of the defense action occurs; in the worst case, the competition of two or more contrasting movements leads to absolute paralysis.

One more reason to think very hard about what to train. To say it clearly: I absolutely don't have any problem with kata (forms), stylized systems for moving meditation or martial arts in the classical meaning as a means for personal perfection. Just the opposite—I have great respect for these systems and the people who perform them. I am merely warning of making the mistake of regarding the techniques trained there as techniques for defense.

Therefore, in the Anglo-American realm a distinction exists between "martial art" and "combat system." Unfortunately, the trend tends toward each school offering the full program of self-discovery, health program, martial art, and self-defense. The reasons for this are mainly the fight for market share and egotism.

But let's come back to the problems of "natural versus trained techniques": from what I already said, it should be clear that a functioning defense system should use as many natural gross motor concepts of movements as possible in order to be able to use them under stress.

7.3. BLADE SYSTEMS

In the previous chapters we have already seen that blades have special characteristics that make them look especially well suited as weapons for defense. But you also have to take into account that blades are not as forgiving of your own mistakes as are impact weapons or your bare hands. These mistakes could be, for example, to injure the attacker much more severely than intended or to hurt yourself. The art of defense with a knife consists less of warding off the attacker than in the ability not to cut yourself in the process.

Many systems for training knife fights work with long or shorter sticks. The stick is in the center of the training and the system. But it is wrong to believe that the stick techniques can simply be translated into blade techniques. Motion patterns, behavior of the weapon, impingement dynamics on the body, the physical situation at impact, the mechanics . . . all of this is slightly different. And just here is the peril: whoever has never or only sometimes used blades in training can't expect to be proficient in using them.

The logical connection between different weapon types is a hierarchical system, at the top of which is the blade. All techniques and concepts that can be

performed successfully and are riskless can be transferred to the stick. And whatever can be performed with the stick can also be transferred to the bare hands.

But this is only a "one-way street" that works safely only in the direction from blade to stick to bare hands. By far, not all the things that work with a stick will work with a blade. A very simplified but plausible example is that, of course, you can hold the stick in front of your opponent's neck and, while standing behind him or her, grasp the stick with both hands and pull your opponent down. With a blade, in contrast, a couple of your fingers would end up on the ground.

Admittedly, the differences between the concepts of blade and stick are usually somewhat more subtle. Especially inveterate stick technicians, at the beginning, have great problems with blades. This does not at all mean that I want to depreciate stick systems and their users. Indeed, they often have an outstanding repertoire and a great variety of techniques. But for defense I prefer the focus to be on a few functioning concepts that can be transferred from the blade to all other tools. This way I can be sure that all the performed techniques work for sure—regardless of what I hold in my hands while under stress.

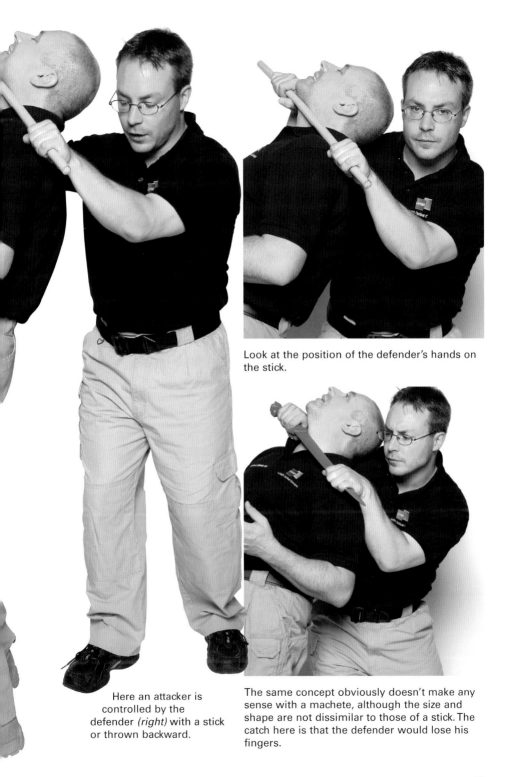

Look at the position of the defender's hands on the stick.

Here an attacker is controlled by the defender *(right)* with a stick or thrown backward.

The same concept obviously doesn't make any sense with a machete, although the size and shape are not dissimilar to those of a stick. The catch here is that the defender would lose his fingers.

73

CHAPTER EIGHT
STANCE, KNIFE GRIP, AND MOVEMENT

8.1. THE CORRECT STANCE

There are at least as many quarrels about the correct stance as there are about politics. Especially at the beginning, you should not think too much about the correct stance, because this only impedes the natural flow of movements. Of course, it makes sense to stand firmly and to stay mobile in every direction. This is best achieved when your feet are about a shoulder's width apart. The toes generally face forward; the backmost foot usually stands a bit more natural if it is turned slightly outward.

Your body weight is not exactly evenly distributed: about 60 to 70 percent of it should rest on the backmost leg. This way you stand firmly while at the same time being able to quickly get out of the opponent's reach by moving sideways or to the back.

It is a matter of taste which leg is in front. If you are right-handed, it makes sense to have your right hand as well as your right leg in front. This way your tool (knife) is always between your body and that of the attacker. Thus the blade (or better, the blade tip) always points at the source of danger, and the opponent first has to get around the blade in order to hit you.

Even though it may look more dangerous in movies, it makes no sense to protect the knife with your left hand, thus moving the free hand forward—in this case your free hand is not protected against your opponent's attack. Your weapon hand can protect itself, because any attack on the weapon is a high risk for your opponent. A slight turn of your wrist, and your blade hits the attacking extremity.

You lift your free hand for cover. In traditional styles, the hand often is put on the chest. But you can also hold it close to the edge of your jaw, like a boxer, or hold it loosely at the same height as your chin or neck area. The free hand takes over tasks such as controlling the opponent's extremities or their weapon arm, or securing open spaces. In an emergency it can also be your last protection measure; for example, by bringing your hand or arm in between the opponent's weapon and your neck. This, of course, should not become a habit, but in an emergency it is better to have your fingers cut off than to receive a cut into the carotid artery.

Turn your upper torso a bit in order not to stand directly in front of the opponent, but a bit sideways. This way you make attacks to vital targets more difficult and offer a smaller area for attack. If you aren't knotted up by now, try not to straighten your knees, but to stand with hips and knees relaxed.

But theory is theory. The stance described here is just the ideal case, and such cases are rather rare in reality. Probably the attack will surprise you, and you will more likely stumble than stand. This doesn't matter; just try to practice this as well! This means that at the beginning, practice techniques starting off with an ideal stance, but then as soon as possible train without watching your stance. Just put the other leg in front, stand extremely broadly or with your legs extremely close together, train out of a run, or start with a stumble. The forms of training you will come to know later will quickly teach you not to stay immobile.

It is important to let yourself be guided by the blade. Don't cling to inflexible standards but develop a feel for the course of the blade. If you listen to your gut feelings, you will realize that certain movements feel natural and happen almost by themselves. Each time something feels strange or tense, you should work on it—

until you feel that your body does exactly what the blade requires of it. It is a big advantage of training with weapons that many movements just arise naturally.

The same is true for combinations of techniques. Don't make the mistake of learning combinations by heart and then using them compulsively. The attack ought to trigger an almost instinctive reaction in you and bring you into a distinctive position. From this position, usually one optimal possibility arises to execute your countertechniques, as well as a couple of less good ones and many bad ones. Just follow these principles, and the applications unfold by themselves.

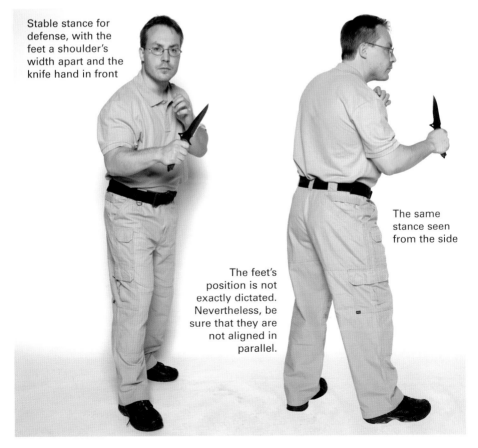

Stable stance for defense, with the feet a shoulder's width apart and the knife hand in front

The same stance seen from the side

The feet's position is not exactly dictated. Nevertheless, be sure that they are not aligned in parallel.

8.2. HOW TO HOLD YOUR KNIFE

Ultimately there are exactly two possibilities for holding a knife: either in the "forward grip" or in "reverse grip." With the forward grip, the blade faces upward, which means that it emerges from the hand between thumb and forefinger. In the reverse grip, the blade emerges at the side of your pinky. All the other grip variations are mere stylistic hairsplitting. Regardless of whether these are called saber grip, ice pick grip, "heaven grip," "fencing grip," "pikal," "Filipino grip," or whatever, the blade is either emerging from the hand facing upward or downward.

In a real defense situation, you are under stress and your hands are either sweaty or bloody. The risk of losing your knife is just too high to try any kind of daring feat. Thus hold your knife firmly! If you feel confident, you can start not to clutch your knife tightly but to hold it in a relaxed way. The trick is to be able to make smooth movements without endangering your secure grip. If you have come that far, you can try the kind of grip that is most comfortable for you.

This is true in any case: with all actions, the blade always faces away from your body and toward the attacker ("edge out")! I teach this body posture in the military sector too. The rule is simple: the blade or tip always points toward the attacker, as does the muzzle of a firearm. Nobody would approve of the idea of walking around with the barrel of a firearm facing oneself. So why should they do it with a knife?

If I control the attacker's arm with my weapon, for example by means of linking arms ("hooking"), I also point the blade toward the attacker. Supporters of the "edge-in" posture argue here that the opponent will injure himself or herself when withdrawing his or her arm. But my aim is exactly this: to get the attacker away from me. Why should I hinder him or her from doing so?

Besides, in a confrontation, attacker and defender collide. Especially in this situation I want the blade to be oriented in such a way as to stop the opponent in their forward movement and to cut them by their own pressure. By using the "edge-in" posture, a collision of the adversaries would injure only the defender.

8.3. GRIPPING COMBINATIONS

In the conflict between attacker and defender, only a limited number of possibilities exist with respect to the position and grip of the knife. Both can hold the knife facing forward; this is called "equal forward." The attacker may hold the knife in reverse grip, and the defender in forward grip. Or, conversely, the attacker may hold the knife in forward grip while the defender uses the reverse grip. Both are called "unequal." And last but not least, there is the possibility that both hold their knives in reverse grip, called "equal reverse."

In addition, both adversaries may carry the knife on their left or right sides. From this arise the possibilities we call "perspectives" (Perspectives of Modular):

- **standard**: Right hand against right hand. Here, both parties are of course right-handers.
- **backward**: Left hand against right hand. Here a left-handed **defender is up against a** right-handed attacker (you are the left-hander).

Forward grip

Reverse grip

Edge in: the blade's edge is facing toward the body. This position is for only a few special applications and is not very reasonable for defense.

Edge out: this way the knife is held with the edge facing away from one's own body.

- **mirror image**: Here a left-hander fights against a left-hander. Due to the small percentage of left-handed people in the population, this situation will hardly ever occur in reality. As a training aid, this gives the possibility to incorporate left-handers into the training without any problems. In addition, right-handers can develop an understanding of the movement concepts of left-handers. Moreover, they learn the equilateral concept, which enhances their coordination as well as giving them practice using their left hand. This becomes especially important in case your right hand is injured or blocked.

- **backward-backward**: Here, the defender is right-handed and the attacker is a left-hander.

Would you like to hold a firearm this way? No? Then you should not hold the knife with the edge pointing toward you.

It looks better this way around (even though the knife attacker here stands too close to the shooter for reasons of illustration).

Now, of course, you can combine the different gripping possibilities with the different perspectives. Thus you receive sixteen different possibilities for the constellation in a conflict. These are not thought-up structures to make everything appear as complicated as possible, only categories of possible situations that can occur in reality.

This may sound very theoretical. Nevertheless, this structure is an important aid for a better understanding of concepts of movement. For the moment, just acknowledge this, then make sure that you practice all the modules to be shown later in all their perspectives. This means that you, as well as your partner, change both between hands and grip variants during training. After a short period of time you'll recognize that you no longer have to think about which hand you hold your tool in, or whether the attacker cuts, stabs, or holds the knife in an ice pick grip.

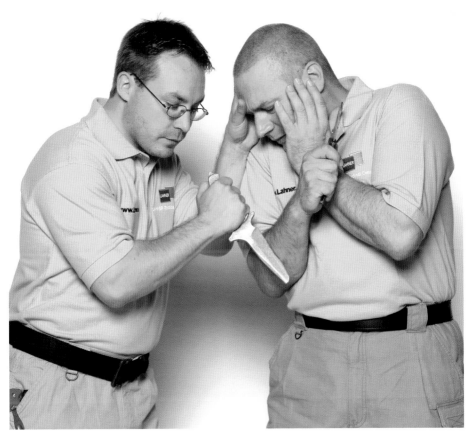

The attacker in any case first has to pass the blade edge. Even a simple impact will result in his wanting to get away from the defender again.

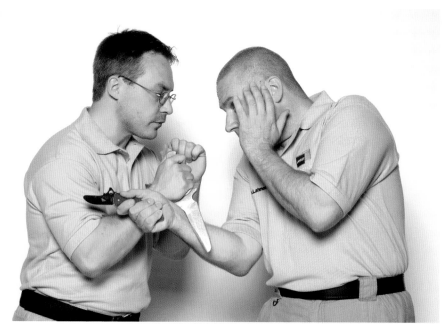

The opponent's weapon arm is held in place for a short time by pressure on the elbow and control at the wrist with the knife. The edge points at the opponent.

If the attacker tries to defend himself by bending the arm, a cut by his own force is the logical consequence.

Here, the blade edge wrongly points at the defender. In reality, the attacker will never work against this forcefully.

Just the opposite: the natural reaction urges a movement away from the pain and thus toward the defender. The attacker is actually invited to continue his attack on the defender. Thus, it is not recommended to hold the blade this way.

8.4. MOVEMENTS

In order to survive a confrontation with knives, you need a lot of movements. The guideline is "Don't be there." Only good footwork and quick movements of the entire body will take you outside the danger zone. The actions of the weapon hand as well as the free hand provide additional safety but should never stand alone by themselves without movement. It has proven to be of value to align footwork and movements along a triangle.

Here, the tip of the triangle can either point away from you or toward you. During the movement, your feet move along the lines of this imaginary triangle. With this form of movement, you achieve two things: first, the movement away from the line of attack and to the inside (in the direction of the attacker's second hand) or toward the outside (and the attacker's back), and second, the movement inside or outside the radius of the attacker's weapon. Ultimately, you are safe only if you are far enough away from the attacker. The movement doesn't always have to be backward but can even lead within the reach of the attacker.

A good exercise for training the footwork in this form and becoming a bit more agile is by practicing the change of steps along a triangle of tape on the ground. At first, stand with your feet on both corners of the triangle's baseline. Then put your right foot forward, toward the triangle's tip. After that, put your left foot on the point where your right foot was before. In this way you first moved forward (to within the attacker's reach) and then turned toward the left.

Now put your left foot back toward its starting point on the left corner of the triangle and afterward put your right foot back to its initial position.

Now do the same thing toward the other side. First put your left foot to the tip of the triangle, then move up with your right foot to where your left foot was at first. At the same time turn to the right. You move back to the neutral starting position by first putting the right foot and then the left one back to their initial positions.

With all movements, it is good not to change your body's center of gravity too much. You achieve this by not lifting your feet completely from the ground, but by dragging the ball of your foot along the ground instead. In addition, you should stand with your feet apart the same distance prior to as well as after each action, as if you had only done a translational movement of your body.

All this may seem a bit jerky and forced. Nobody will actually require you to walk exactly along these points on a triangle. But this exercise shows you an optimized form of movements that, in principle, you can resort to later. You will learn further concepts and principles of movement in the following chapters.

Here, too, it is true: don't ruminate too much about your footwork, but instead let your movements be guided by your blade. Later, when you feel more confident, you can refine your footwork.

Grip combinations: equal forward

Unequal

Unequal

Equal reverse

Perspectives of the Modular System: the views that an observer has of the possible combinations of attacks and defensive actions led with the right and left hands. Here: standard (right against right).

Backward

Mirror image

Backward-backward

A movement away from the attacker's knife doesn't have to be necessarily backward. A movement toward the attacker is very effective and tactically of advantage.

Starting position for training: both feet are at the
base of the triangle.

The right foot is put toward the apex and turned inward slightly.

The left foot moves toward the other corner of the base.

The left foot moves back to its initial position.

Completely back at the initial stance

Now the left foot moves toward the tip of the triangle.

The right one follows by changing to the other corner of the base.

And back in reverse order

Back at the initial position

CHAPTER NINE
THE DIFFERENT ANGLES

To make learning and also practice easier, it makes sense to introduce a nomenclature. This doesn't have to be a giant terminology of terms, but it improves communication to first explain some expressions.

For a successful defense against attacks, it is imperative to realize from which direction the attack is coming. The fewer variants you have to take into account here, the quicker a reaction to the attack can happen. In order to systematize the recognition of attacks and to simplify communication in training, the attacks are classified according to their angles. Here, the exact target of the attack and the exact execution are not relevant.

Attack no. 1, for example, follows the approximate path of movement for a slap in the face. Seen from your point of view as a defender, the attacker strikes out with his right hand and hits from the upper left to the lower right, in the direction of your head and neck area. This attack still has the same number in case you actively start the same technique as a counterattack (from your point of view, from the right side toward the left, using your right arm).

So, if you strike out with your right hand and hit a "forehand" to the area of the attacker's neck or head, this is also a number 1. Thus, in training there won't be any discussions about which angle is meant by number 1.

Even more important is that with this way of numbering, you also have the possibility of classifying attacks during a defense situation. The normal defense process first requires realizing the angle. When you have seen this, you have to choose one out of the possible reactions. After this, your body has to perform this response to the attack.

This means that a lot of time is necessary for analyzing the attack and choosing your answer to it. If you try to distinguish not

A cut with angle no. 1 as you would see it during an attack

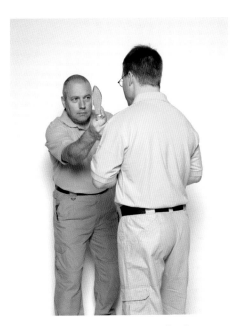

The same cut; here, during application

The same angle no. 1 led with the left hand. There is no difference for you with respect to direction and path in space.

In comparison, here it doesn't matter for the angle whether the knife is held with the left or right hand.

only between the direction and angle of the attack but also whether, for example, it is made with the palm, the edge of hand, the closed fist, the stick, the knife (here you have to distinguish between forward and reverse grip), or a rusty chain, the analysis will continue endlessly. That way, no successful defense is possible.

Conversely, it is problematic to generalize all attacks up to a point where the defender has only a single standard reply in his or her repertoire. This way you will never allow for all the degrees of danger—especially with knife attacks. It is not sufficient only to distinguish between an attack coming from the left or right. At a minimum you must also note whether the attack is coming in high or in the area of your neck or is instead aimed toward your belly.

Angle no. 1

The Modular System, with its system of numbers, offers a good concept. The attacks are classified according to categories that enable quick reaction but are nevertheless sufficiently differentiated. Here, the numbers relate only to the angle of attack. It is not of importance for the defense whether the attack is made by a right-hander or left-hander. It also doesn't matter which weapon or which kind of grip is used for the attack.

You surely remember our "one-way street" in the hierarchy of weapons. Since we always assume that the attacker uses a knife, we cover the worst-case scenario with this assumption. You only have to react the way you will learn in the following exercises. But if the attack is made only with a stick or with the bare hands, you will be on the safe side by applying your standard answer.

In the photos on this and the following page you can see the attack angles from numbers 1 through 5 and the angle number 12. I won't discuss the numbers 6 through

Angle no. 2

Angle no. 3

Angle no. 4

Angle no. 5

Angle no. 12

11 in the scope of this book, since they represent only more-differentiated variants that are not necessary for basic defense.

In these images you see your opponent. For training, take a stable stance, with both legs parallel. For cover, take your left hand up to your chin or put it on your chest. Take the knife into your right hand with a forward grip and follow with your knife the angles and cutting lines on the images from 1 to 12. These exercises are nothing but shadow boxing, by which you practice your techniques with an imaginary opponent. Your movement no. 1 is made (seen from your point of view) from the upper right outside toward the lower left inside. During this movement, your arms move from an open into a closed position.

For your footwork there are several possibilities: you can either move your right leg forward even more during cutting, while your upper torso turns to the right, or you move your left leg backwards Both variants result in the same position.

You will see that your arms are usually quicker than your legs. To solve this problem, you can rotate your hip while standing on the balls of your feet only. For this you make a movement as if dancing the "twist." With a cut along angle no. 1, this way your right hip comes forward and your left side moves backward. This results in your upper torso turning left. Just experiment with these different footwork options and find out the best one for you.

The cut along angle no. 2 is done with your backhand from the upper left to the lower right. The target here, too, is the head or your opponent's neck area. Your body again should turn to the right. Your arms have opened again.

No. 3 is done horizontally to the area of the belly from the right outside, again by turning your body.

Hip movement at no. 1, starting position

The knife moves over the body's center.

End position of the movement

Starting position for angle no. 2

The turn of the hip moves the knife across the centerline.

End position of no. 2

Angle no. 1 with a turn by footwork, starting position

The leg on the same side as the knife (in this case, on the right) moves to the front.

The leg on the opposite side (here, on the left) moves backward and the end position is achieved.

From there it continues with angle no. 2; the right leg is taken back.

The left leg moves to the front.

The right leg moves backward to the rear.

No. 4 occurs at the same level but in the opposite direction, from left to right.

No. 5 is a straight cut toward the belly.

No. 12, finally, is a vertical movement from top to bottom toward the attacker's head.

Please, take into account that no. 12 can be done in two different ways. Either you can move your right hand from top to bottom on the right side of your body, or you can do it on your body's left side.

Now practice the cuts 1 through 5 and 12 in a successive flow, without stopping in between. You will see that the coasting movement of one cut is at the same time the strikeout movement of the next one. Your body moves, from the hip upward, alternately to the left and right. At the same time, your arms move from an open to a closed position and back toward an

No. 12 on the outside, passing the right side of the body

Angle no. 12 on the inside (i.e., on the body's left side downward to the left leg)

open one. It is important to understand this principle because the countermoves result from this.

Because of its anatomical structure, the human body has only a limited number of possibilities for moving. As you have just seen, you can open your arms (as if you wanted to hug somebody) or you can close your arms (as if you wanted to hug yourself). You can do this horizontally or vertically and also alternating (one arm open, the other closed) or at the same time.

With this, by and large, the variants of moving the upper torso are described. Surely you remember what I told you about natural gross motor movements. The concepts of movements described above are innate or otherwise learned in early childhood and are gross motor skills. No. 1 corresponds to an instinctive hitting movement or protective reaction with crossing the centerline (the vertical line running through fontanel, nose, larynx, solar plexus, and genitals). No. 12 is nothing but lifting the arms. For example, this is done instinctively for protection, with subsequent dropping of them.

Now take the knife into your left hand. Nothing is changed. Regardless of holding the knife in your left or right hand, a cut along angle no. 1 stays an angle no. 1. If you cut a no. 1 with your right hand, this is a forehand movement. With the left hand this becomes a backhand movement. This means that a number 1 with the left hand again has to be done from the upper right to the lower left. You can see this most clearly by holding a knife in each hand. Focus on your right hand but move the left hand with it in parallel. This way the movements of your left hand become clear quickly.

These basic variants of movement exist for the upper torso and arms: opening the arms horizontally.

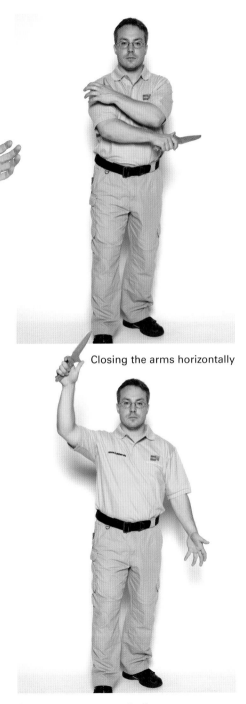

Closing the arms horizontally

Opening the arms vertically

Closing the arms vertically

Alternating movements horizontally

Simultaneous lifting vertically

Simultaneous dropping vertically

Angle no. 1 with the left hand

Angle no. 2

Angle no. 3

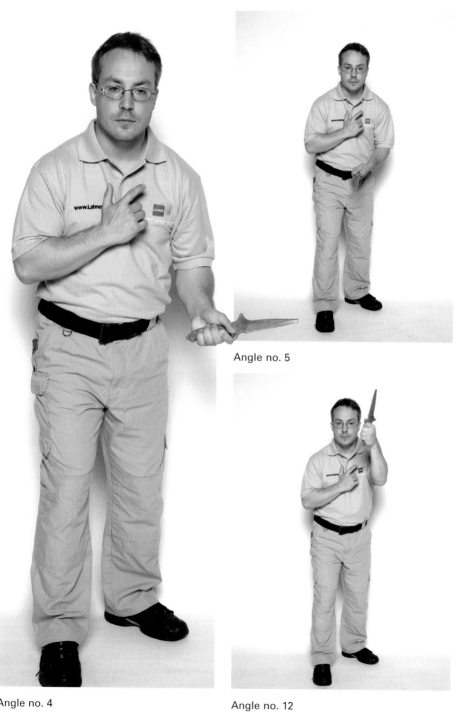

Angle no. 5

Angle no. 4

Angle no. 12

Angle no. 1 with two knives. It doesn't matter in which hand the knife is.

Angle no. 2 with two knives

CHAPTER TEN
THE CLOSED KNIFE

In particular, folders have the great advantage that they can also be used for noncutting functions. With these knives, you can defend yourself against attacks that legally as well as ethically are distinctly below the escalation level of a real knife confrontation.

The closed knife is ideal for hitting, pushing, and pressing on nerve points. Although I don't believe in the applicability of real pressure points under stress by fast-moving opponents, it is nevertheless clear that there are special spots on the human body that are very sensitive to pressure or hits. While these points have to be hit very precisely with bare hands, a tool such as a closed folder can compensate for inaccuracy created by the fight. It is already sufficient to hit the approximate spot of a pressure or nerve point.

The knives of Bram Frank are especially made for effective use in a closed state. But every other knife, as well as items of daily use, such as ballpoint pens or keys, can be used in this way. Thus, in the descriptions in this part of the book, you can replace the closed knife with any other suitable item or even the bare hand. Even an open folder or fixed blade can be used in a noncutting way for hitting or pressing, in the event that it fits the situation.

Hit onto the arm with closed knife to break the grip

10.1. DEFENSE AGAINST STRANGLING ATTACK

"Strangling" as a sole means of attack is rather a romantic dream of any martial artist, because he or she can easily fend it off. Indeed, an attacker would be quite stupid to have both hands at one point (the neck) while the other person has both hands free to defend himself or herself. Thus, strangling attacks are often accompanied by attacks of another kind or serve to intimidate. It is not rare for the defender to be grabbed at the throat and pressed against a wall, while the second hand of the attacker is drawing a weapon.

If you, as a defender, spend too much time on levering or other forceful actions in this situation, you run the risk of getting hit by the weapon. On the other hand, it is of course impossible to immediately draw your knife and to cut as soon as someone touches your neck. In this case, it is good to draw the knife but use it in closed position. This way the attack can be fended off at a low level of escalation, while opening the knife can be performed quickly at any time. But this shouldn't hide the fact that a determined strangling attack can quickly turn into a threat for your life.

Nevertheless, we want to demonstrate the classic strangling attack and its defense with an example—because it is so cool.

The attacker strangles with both hands and pushes the defender backward. So that he or she doesn't go down, the defender stabilizes the stance by moving one leg backward.

Strangling attacks lose part of their power when the defender pulls his shoulders upward and draws the chin to the chest. Then the defender pushes the palm of his hand toward the attacker's face. This way the forward movement is stopped and some time is won to draw the knife. This

is very important, because otherwise the process of drawing can be recognized and blocked by the attacker.

Afterward the defender hits the attacker's forearm with the knife's handle butt. The target is the forearm on the thumb side, a bit below the crook of the elbow. The hit is continued as pressure until the arm is released from the neck.

If necessary, the assaulter can be further attacked with the handle butt. But hits against the head can result in severe injuries and are necessary only under certain circumstances (for example, several attackers or additional weapons in the match). The substantial bruises left on large muscle groups by hitting with the handle butt should convince most attackers to desist.

10.2. DEFENSE AGAINST PUNCHES AND HOOKS

Hits can't always be warded off as simply and elegantly as it appears in training. Usually you can't recognize where the hit came from. In theory, we distinguish between straight and curved pushes and hits, but this is not very helpful in a wild "tussle."

It makes sense to adopt a kind of "first reaction" that is applied to any kind of hit. This way you avoid being knocked out at the very first hit. With standardized first reactions you avoid the long reaction times created by analyzing the attack and choosing the right defense. But in turn you have to accept that the standardized reaction doesn't always fit exactly to the attack. This disadvantage also prevents its effective use against knives, but this method works well against hits.

There are a number of interesting solutions. Here again we use a natural reaction that is easy to learn as well. People

Firm stance against a strangling grip with both hands

Push toward the face with the ball of one's hand, performed with open hand.

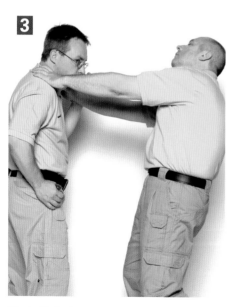

The knife is drawn.

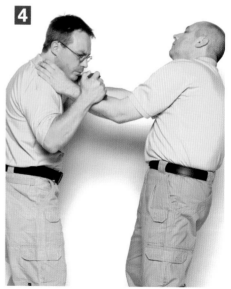

Hit with the handle butt ("butt strike") toward the lower arm

Starting position

"Panic cover position" with movement to the left out of the line of attack

who are attacked tend to protect their head with both arms. If there is still enough time to do it, we draw the knife in the same movement. At the same time we move forward to the left to get out of the opponent's line of attack and to get to his or her outside. This is called "panic cover position."

In the first example the opponent attacks rather straight on. Moving to the left, we let the straight punch pass by. The panic cover position protects the head. Now the free hand secures the attacker's arm in the area of his shoulder or upper arm to prevent further attacks. The weapon hand is now able to hit the upper arm, shoulder, chest muscles, collar bone, or face with hammering movements.

In the second example the attack begins with a hook. Again, we move forward to the left and protect ourselves with the panic cover position. This way we are able to stop the attack at an early point in time, when it still has developed only little energy. Here it is important to go as hard as possible into the attack in order to nip it in the bud. The free hand again prevents

The attacker *(right)* aims straight toward the defender's face.

The defender protects himself by means of the panic cover position and evades toward the left.

With the left (free) arm, the opponent's arm is secured while the knife is drawn at the same time.

Now the handle butt can be used for hammering. Depending on the level of escalation, targets from the arm to the head are possible.

further attacks of your opponent. The weapon hand is now free for counterattacks, pressure, or hits, depending on the situation.

Please take into account that you can also determine the level of escalation by the choice of targets on the attacker's body. For example, you can signal to your opponent by means of a hard blow on the chest that he or she has overstepped a threshold. The same kind of punch to the face can cause severe injuries and thus is used only in corresponding situations. The advantage of a tool is that you can limit yourself to less problematic targets and can achieve a good effect without overly endangering the attacker.

The attacker *(right)* applies a hook.

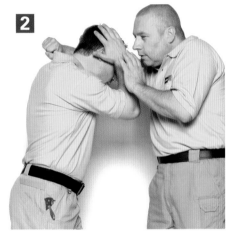

The defender moves into the attack by using the panic cover position and stops the attack early on.

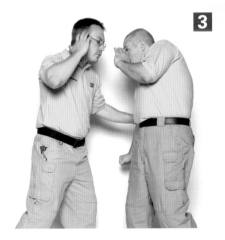

The attacker's hand is briefly immobilized with the left hand.

The counterattack with the ball of one's hand or a hammer blow is done with the right hand.

10.3. SELF-DEFENSE FOR WOMEN

Women should also look into using a knife, since they hardly have a chance in self-defense without any tool—not because all women are weak, but because the definition of a self-defense situation for women contains this as a premise. Remember that a perpetrator always looks for an easy target. This is particularly pronounced when it comes to assaults on women, but when a man is attacked, such as after offensive, rude remarks have spun out of control, a balance of power is still possible. However, when a woman is the target, this is definitely not the case.

Assaults on women are done less out of the need to satisfy the sex drive; the main intention is a demonstration of power. The perpetrator wants to control the victim, to break her, to see her suffering and begging. The decisive incentive for the perpetrator is not the victim's attractiveness but her degree of helplessness. Therefore, he will always choose a woman as a victim who is inferior in physical strength by a mile. Thus, the only really safe way for defense is by using a weapon.

A sequence is shown here that can be executed by any woman. The attacker approaches the defender. She clearly signals him to stop by gestures (palm of the hands facing the attacker) and loud shouting. Nevertheless, the attacker comes closer and tries to grab the woman.

Defensive stance of the defender

The defender draws her knife while her other hand pushes toward the attacker's face, and then she uses the butt of the knife handle to hammer on the attacker's sternum. At the same time the right shoulder and right leg move forward, which means that the defender practically walks into the attacker. Subsequently, she saves herself by running from this situation.

Rape, both in a physical and psychological sense, is extremely brutal and cruel. And afterward there is no guarantee to be spared one's life when the perpetrator realizes the impact of his act and, in panic, tries to control possible consequences. I am sure that if more women knew how helpful knives can be, more women would be using them. In particular, women are able to quickly grasp the concepts of movement and usually have an outstanding feel for their body. For women, it is important to work on reducing their acquired, socialized dread of violence and to internalize that this can be a solution for especially dicey situations.

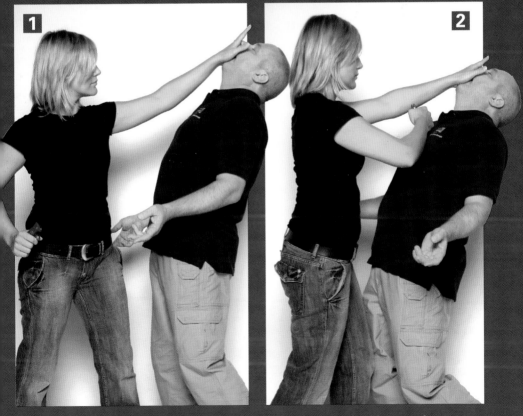

1 Push with the hand toward the face and drawing of the knife.

2 Multiple hammering blows on the sternum

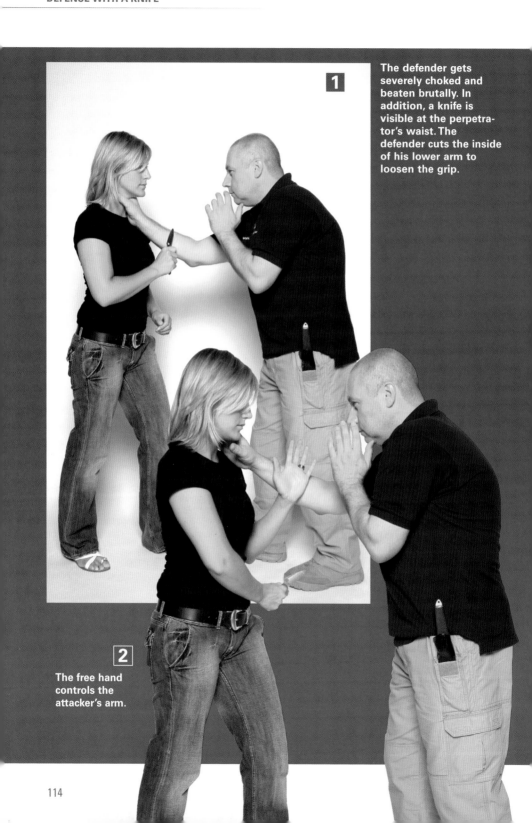

1 The defender gets severely choked and beaten brutally. In addition, a knife is visible at the perpetrator's waist. The defender cuts the inside of his lower arm to loosen the grip.

2 The free hand controls the attacker's arm.

3

A cut across the thigh muscle inhibits the attacker's mobility.

4

The defender is able to escape.

10.4. GRIPPING THE WEAPON ARM

Of course, the attacker can realize that you are drawing your knife, and then he tries to grab your weapon arm. Some simple solutions exist for dealing with this problem.

With Closed Knife

In our example the attacker grabs the weapon arm with the opposite hand. The defender then can immobilize the attacker's hand on his arm by making a circular clockwise movement with his or her weapon arm. A turn of the wrist takes the knife's handle butt to the attacker's wrist. By exerting downward pressure, the defender causes a strong pain to be created that encourages the attacker to let go of the hand.

The simpler variant is to gain a bit more space by hits with the free hand as soon as your weapon arm is grabbed. Simple doesn't mean bad. Just the opposite: everything that is easy functions better when one is under stress.

1

The weapon arm is grabbed with the opposing hand.

2

A circular movement follows with the knife across the attacker's arm.

3

The wrist position during the lock

Since the lever technique more properly belongs to the realm of martial arts, the move is finished with a knee hit.

The attacker (at right) grabs the hand.

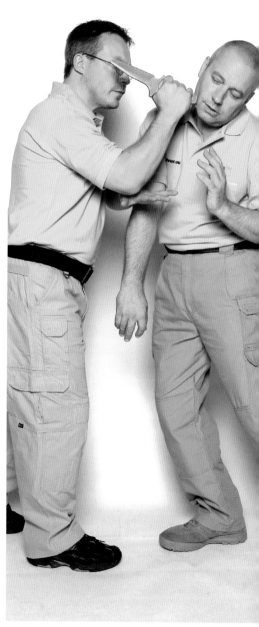

The weapon arm is led upward to loosen the grip.

A hit with the handle butt follows.

With Open Knife

As long as you keep your weapon arm in continuous motion, it is extremely difficult for an attacker to grab your arm without getting cut. If you are grasped nevertheless, the escape move in principle follows the same concept as in the previous example.

But this time you don't fix the attacker's hand and thus are able to cut immediately. Instead, you move your weapon arm clockwise as if you would paint a big circle on the wall with the tip of your blade. The movement of your wrist presses the blade down onto the attacker's arm; the resulting pain and injury to tissue should end in his letting go of you.

Here it is important to apply enough kinetic energy to compensate for probable advantages of the attacker with respect to his or her force in the initial phase. For this, the body follows the path of the blade by turning the upper torso to the right. You achieve this by moving the right leg backward or by putting the left leg forward.

Here, too, a simple but very effective variant exists: extending the free hand toward the attacker's face in order to make the attacker let go. As soon as your own weapon arm is grasped by the attacker, you pull it toward you and upward while at the same time doing a counterattack toward his face with your open hand. The opponent's arm is controlled to give you a moment of safety. If necessary, you can now hit the attacker's face with the knife handle or fist. If required by the situation, the cutting use of your tool is possible anytime.

You can see that a knife doesn't always have to be used for cutting. Personally, I don't see any problem in drawing a knife during a confrontation as long as you don't use it as such. But this requires good training to prevent you from using the blade hastily in a panic.

Most of the lever techniques taught in martial arts mainly work in training—but not against an aggressive attacker on the street, who doesn't think of keeping immobile until you have found the right grip. Here, a blunt tool (e.g., closed folder, ballpoint pen, flashlight) is very useful.

The simple rule for use is this: attack the exact source of the actual danger. If, for example, a hand comes into your personal safety zone, hit the hand with your knife handle. If somebody kicks you, hit on the lower leg or thigh. Keep your cover high and wait for the attacker to stretch and thus expose himself or herself. If you have hit the attacking extremity, you can use the effect of the hit and either run away or approach closer to the attacker.

A frequent—and well-founded—point for criticism with respect to hits on the extremities is that the effect is too small. We have to be clear about the effect of such hits (in contrast to cuts) being dependent mainly on the pain reaction of the attacker. All techniques that depend on pain are usable only if the situation allows such a low level of escalation without taking a high risk.

In addition, it is recommended to be prepared for the possibility that the opponent doesn't show the desired reaction because he or she is drugged or drunk, has too much adrenaline in the blood, or simply is not very sensitive to pain. However, I find it unnecessary and legally questionable to forego the techniques of the low-escalation level and to always and immediately go whole hog. With a certain repertoire you can use the entire bandwidth of escalation levels and fully utilize all options.

Grabbing the hand

The blade is moved across the attacker's arm this way.

Strike to the attacker's arm to speed up loosening of the grip

4

Threatening with the knife (if necessary). As an alternative, a cut toward the shoulder is performed, if the attacker tries to reach for his own weapon.

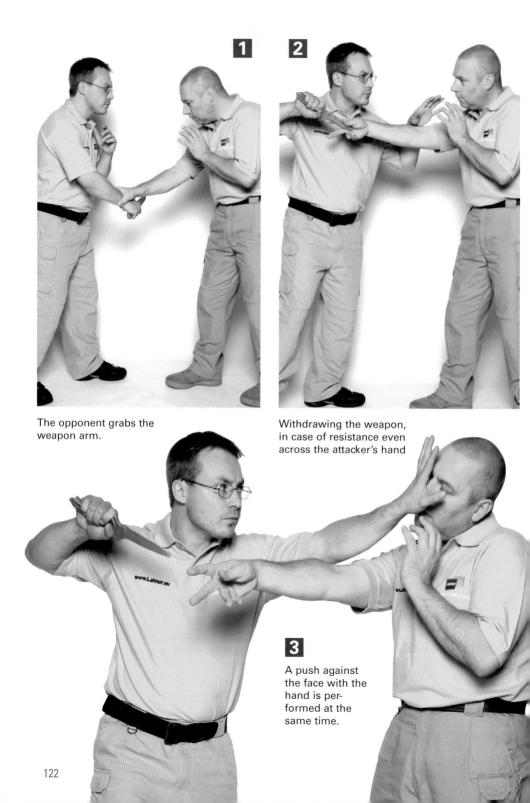

The opponent grabs the weapon arm.

Withdrawing the weapon, in case of resistance even across the attacker's hand

A push against the face with the hand is performed at the same time.

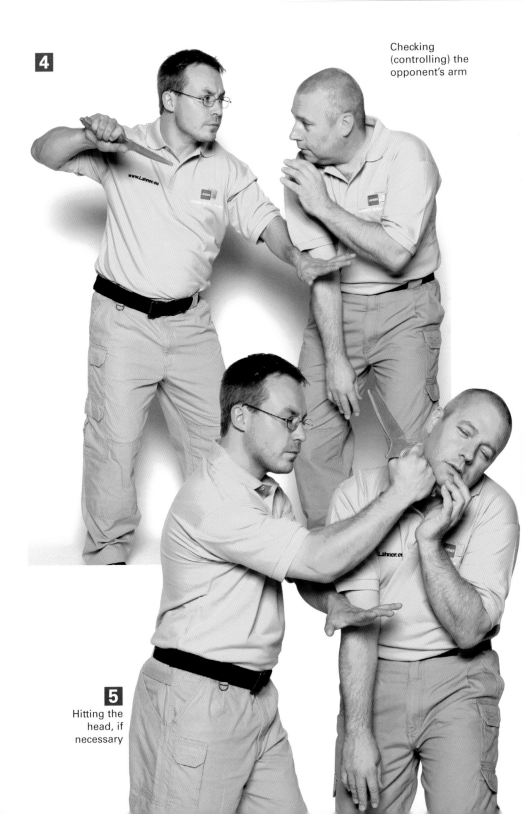

4

Checking (controlling) the opponent's arm

5
Hitting the head, if necessary

CHAPTER ELEVEN
MODULES AND APPLICATIONS

In this chapter I will introduce the individual modules of the Modular System. These always contain three attacks and their corresponding defense. In addition, each module contains the training of specific components, such as movements, footwork, or lines of attack.

Because of their cyclic structure, you can practice the modules endlessly. If you train with a partner, the roles of attacker and defender are continually alternating. This means that your partner attacks, you fend off the attack, and your counterattack is already an attack on your partner. Put somewhat simpler, this means that your partner attacks as a "baddie" while you defend yourself as a "good guy." As soon as you have repelled the attack, you turn into a "baddie" and your counterattack is the attack on your partner, who is now the "good guy." It is imperative and typical in the Modular System that the baddie attacks the neck and torso while the goody applies only biomechanical cuts to the extremities.

You remember that it is important to stop the attack as quickly as possible. For tactical, legal, and ethical reasons, you as a defender work only on the extremities. Never cut the neck or the torso!

As soon as you are able to perform a module smoothly and without mistakes, you can transfer the learned concepts into practice. An important principle in training is to practice slowly, consciously, and with control and also to think about what you are doing. If you perform the module (or

the "drill" as it is called in the Philippine martial arts) only semiautomatically and race through it, this looks very impressive but is of no use.

You always have to stop the attack first and in a hard way. Only then do you continue in a less forceful way. This change from hard to dialed-down is not entirely easy, but decisive. Many people in training can "get cut" during the drill with a bit of pressure and intention, although they are performing the right movements. It is often the case that their defense is not hard enough. But if you don't get this right, even the prettiest subsequent movement doesn't help you at all!

The modules are always named after the attack they contain. Module "1-4-12," for example, trains the student in attacks 1, 4, and 12 as well as their respective defense. Count the numbers out loud while practicing. This helps you focus on the current technique. Count together with your training partner: "1, 4, 12." And again, "1, 4, 12."

11.1. MODULE 1-4-12

Module 1-4-12 is the basic module and serves as a foundation for all the others. At the same time it deals with the most-frequent kinds of attack. It teaches you a feel for body rotation and shows possibilities for warding off attacks. In addition, you learn the use of your second hand for controlling and checking.

A small preliminary exercise (no real application!) makes the later movement easier: let your training partner hold his or her knife at the left side of your neck. Now rotate on the balls of your feet in such a way that your position is in front of your opponent's weapon arm. By doing this, you bring your knife to your partner's forearm. At the same time, by means of the rotation, your neck and head should have moved away from your partner's knife.

Just think of dancing the "twist" while rotating your hips. Here it is important that you move sideways away from the attacker's knife, while at the same time intruding into the partner's radius for attacking.

Practice this slowly and repeatedly. During this drill, you should turn sideways and away from the knife while at the same time moving toward your partner. When you are proficient in this, you can finally pull out all the stops.

11.1.1. THE STANDARD VERSION OF MODULE 1-4-12

With this we come to the complete module 1-4-12. First the attacker charges with a no. 1 (similar to a slap in the face) toward the defender's neck. The defender has to stop the incoming attack as quickly as possible. To do this, he or she stops the attacker's weapon arm with his or her knife. So as not to be hit in the area of the head, he or she creates some distance by turning the body (on the balls of their feet or by means of footwork). Here, it is important to go into the radius of attack by means of a turn. Please be sure not only to scratch your opponent's attacking arm but, indeed, to stop its movement.

Next, you cut the flexors on the inside forearm of the weapon arm. While doing so, pull the knife back toward your left hip and be sure that the knife tip still points toward the attacker, in order to keep him

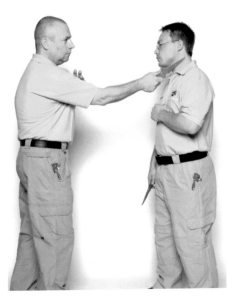

Preliminary exercise: the training knife is at right at the defender's neck.

A rotation of the hip and feet toward the left follows.

or her at a distance. By executing this cut, in reality the attacker's grip on his or her knife should distinctly loosen; perhaps even his or her fist opens and the knife drops to the ground.

Since no guarantee can be given for a complete biomechanical stop, due to the presence of clothing and the imprecision of the hit, simply put the knife back by your arm. As soon as the knife leaves the

Seen from above: knife at the neck

The rotation takes the defender out of reach.

opponent's forearm after cutting, the back of your hand or outside forearm takes control over the opponent's weapon arm. If the knife should still be in his or her hand, you have a guard for your neck.

By this point in the drill you have learned some very important items: first, you have seen that it is your tool that first reacts to the attack. This principle is relatively safe to carry out, because this way you don't have to intercept a knife in motion with your bare hands. If the attacker draws back quickly right after the attack, he or she will cut themselves on your knife but in no case will injure your arm. The principle for warding off this kind of attack

is this: first the knife, then the hand, also called "cut and check."

Before you continue, you have to make sure that the attack has been stopped for the moment. While you will learn in later applications to continue as a defender at this point, in this exercise you will now exchange the roles of attacker and defender.

You, as a new attacker, will now cut with a no. 4 horizontally to your partner's belly. Because his knife is still farther up, for him the quickest possibility to stop the attack is to stretch his free arm downward. This way, attack no. 4 stops at the partner's forearm.

Your partner now drops his knife arm and cuts over the back of your knife hand. At the same time he moves his right leg to the back to remove his body from the reach of your knife. Here your partner uses the principle in reverse order: first the hand, then the knife—"check and cut."

The cut on the back of the hand doesn't lead to the fist being opened, because at this point no group of muscles or tendons responsible for opening the fist is within reach. If possible, try to cut the thumb in order to weaken the grip on the knife.

With this, the attack is stopped and the roles of attacker and defender change again. The cut toward the weap-

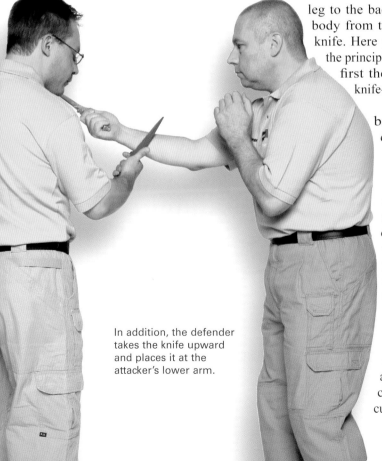

In addition, the defender takes the knife upward and places it at the attacker's lower arm.

on arm is continued backward by your partner and results in an attack no. 12 toward your head. In accordance with the principle "first the knife, then the hand," you stop the attack with your blade in a maneuver called the "umbrella block." Here, the tip of your knife faces to the left.

Now your free hand pushes into the created space between both weapon arms. You can combine this movement with a stab to the eyes or a push with the flat hand toward the face. Your free hand makes sure that in case of an intrusion into your block, the attacker's

Attack with angle no. 1 by partner *A (at right)*.

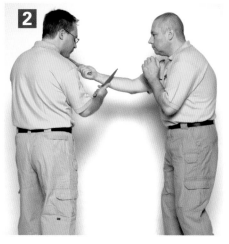

B (left) turns as in the previous exercise and stops the weapon arm hard with his knife.

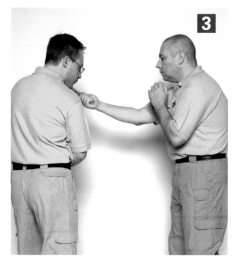

He cuts across the inside of the lower arm toward his left hip.

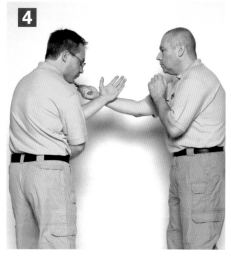

B checks *A*'s arm with his free hand.

arm glides along yours toward the left side of your body.

As soon as the attack is stopped, you glide forward and to the right, out of the line of attack. During this you make your countercut to the opponent's arm. The accompanying footwork is mostly up to you. I recommend here to glide in a way as described in section 14.1, on footwork.

The three attacks included in this module are now successfully completed. Now you can start an attack no. 1 yourself without any break.

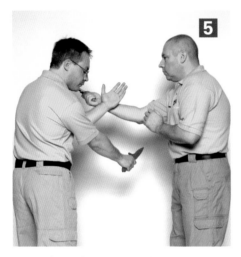

Now *B (at left)* cuts toward *A*'s belly with a no. 4.

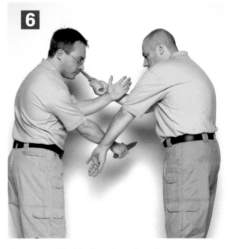

A stops with his free hand and turns away from the attack.

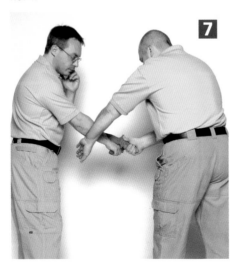

Then *A* cuts across *B*'s weapon arm.

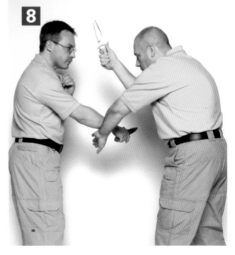

Afterward, *A* starts a counterattack no. 12 toward the head of *B*.

Umbrella block: *B* lifts his blade and stops *A*'s attack hard.

B pushes his left arm forward underneath his weapon arm and toward the face of *A*.

B evades to the right, cutting the attacking arm as well with this step.

This ends the first half of the drill. Now *B* attacks with a no. 1.

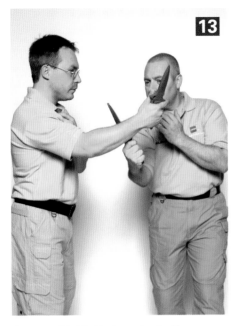

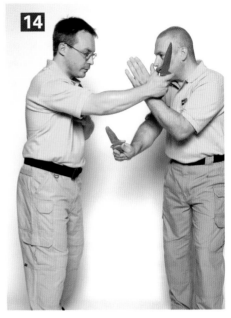

A stops with his blade and cuts *B*'s arm.

A checks with his free hand.

A attacks with no. 4, which is stopped by *B* with his arm.

B cuts over the hand of the stopped arm holding the weapon.

B performs an angle no. 12 toward A's head.

A lifts his blade and stops B with it.

He moves the free arm to the front.

20

A cuts *B* at his weapon arm and evades to the right.

21

With this, the drill is completed and *A* can start with no. 1 again.

Typical mistake: don't stop attack no. 4 with the palm of your hand facing downward!

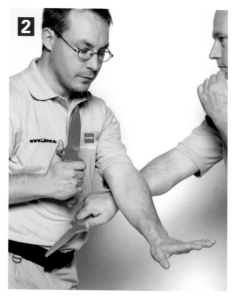

If you are too late or the attacker slides through, he arrives at your body.

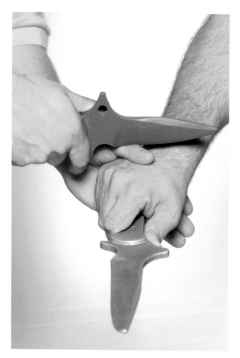

A grip with the thumb at the attacker's back of hand is problematic too, because you may cut your thumb.

When fending off an attack no. 12 (here performed by the partner on the left), take care of the following:

2

If the defender (right) pushes the weapon arm downward zestfully with his free hand . . .

3

. . . the attacker (left) may use this in order to cut toward the body.

You will realize that after two complete repetitions, each of you was in the position of attacker and defender with respect to all three angles. Practice this module slowly, exactly, and with concentration. You should know at each point in the exercise whether you have the role of attacker or defender and where your hand and knife are. You protect yourself from cuts with your own knife by trying to move your free hand and your knife hand in opposite directions or at least in parallel.

As soon as you learn to perform the movements more fluidly, you will have a lot of fun with this exercise. But please keep in mind that this is an exercise and in no way is it the real thing.

11.1.2. USES OF 1-4-12

You have just learned techniques for fending off the most-common kinds of attack. Now turn the skills you learned in the module into defense scenarios that

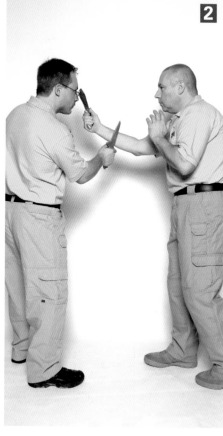

Application: the attacker (right) aims toward the neck with no. 1.

The defender (left) stops the attack with the blade as in module 1-4-12.

are more realistic. For this, you disasso-ciate the movements of the drill and transfer them into scenarios that are close to reality.

The attacker charges with a cut to the neck (attack no. 1). As before, you stop the attack with your knife, check with your left hand, and cut the flexors of the forearm.

In the module, at this point an attack no. 4 toward the belly would follow. Indeed, you can also perform this in reality as a counterattack, but you would do this a bit

farther downward on the body, cutting the front of the attacker's thigh instead.

Here you see that as required by bio-mechanical cutting, your counterattack is performed at the attacker's extremity. Nevertheless, the principle of movement of module 1-4-12 is followed, and you answer an attack no. 1 with an angle no. 4. Except for the target, nothing has changed.

You can now either escape or, accord-ing to the principle of opening and closing the arms, add further cuts to the opponent.

3

He cuts the weapon arm and checks with the free hand.

4

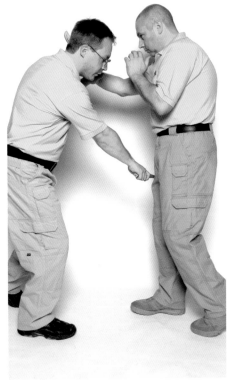

Counterattack no. 4 (following in the module here) is applied biomechanically on the thigh instead of the belly.

The best option: escape, if possible

Alternative: after the cut toward the thigh follows a no. 1 toward the attacker's arm

Afterward, there follows a cut no. 4 toward the left leg.

Here you can see that the thigh's front side is cut at the muscle. An injury of the artery deep on the inside has to be avoided.

With this you should learn that it's not the exact target that is important, but the angle and the level of movement. A horizontal backhand toward the belly is, in concept, an attack no. 4, as is a horizontal backhand toward the thigh.

In the module you have seen that the quickest way to start a counterattack from the defense of attack no. 1 is to work horizontally from your hip. This follows the natural principle of movement of "open your arms / close your arms," which means that the uses follow from the modules. All you have to do is to react to the attack and then automatically let the module run. A reaction to attack no. 1 with "cut and check" by closing the arms can thus be done only by opening the arms.

Here you can't cut toward the attacker's upper torso because there is not enough space between you and the attacker when you clash, and you would inevitably cut yourself by changing from the area of the legs to the area of the upper torso.

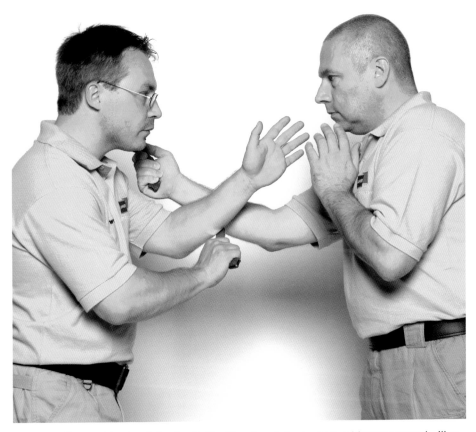

Warding off a no. 1 by the defender *(left)* with cut and check—here a bit exaggerated—illustrates the closeness of check arm and blade. An upward counterattack entails the risk of cutting oneself. The path downward is the only choice.

If you stay within the module's course of action and don't come up with a completely new defense combination, you will be able to stop the attack reflexively and without hesitation and immediately do a counterattack. By frequently practicing the modules, this is done instinctively. In addition, the module optimally combines stopping the attack and initiating a counterattack. This way you can't cut yourself, you move efficiently, and you take the shortest way.

Back to our first simple application: if the attacker loses the knife as a result of the cut or pulls back his or her arm, you have a good chance for escape. Cut no. 4 toward the thigh makes sure that the attacker can't follow you. This way you responded to a potentially lethal attack to your neck in a relatively mild way. Nevertheless, you have not taken an increased risk but have protected yourself as well as the attacker.

Cut toward the shoulder with angle no. 1

Critics often doubt the effectiveness of biomechanical cutting. At this point, it has to be clear that every defense needs an analysis of its success. In no case are you allowed to turn around and run off without making sure that the attacker no longer poses a threat. Otherwise you may end up with a knife in your back.

If the knife is still in the attacker's hand and your cut to the thigh doesn't seem to have achieved the desired result, continue to work until the attack is stopped. But keep in mind that impairing the attacker's func-

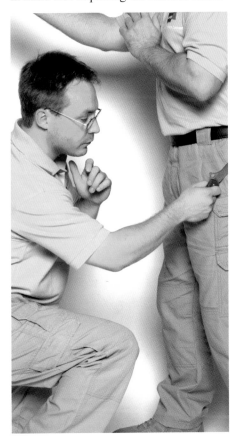

The no. 1 deep toward the leg. From the viewpoint of the defender *(left)*, this is no other movement than toward the neck, as in the module.

tion achieves better and quicker results than the attempt to kill the attacker.

Thus, if the attacker's inability to fight is not yet accomplished, further techniques may look like the following ones. Here, too, try to recognize the parallels to the basic module and analyze the movements. Figure out why the shown movements are especially advantageous or how they unfold.

Since your arms are open after attack no. 4 toward the thigh, close them again. Make a cut at angle no. 1 toward the weapon arm. The no. 1, which finds its way to the neck in the module, thus turns into no. 1 to the arm, the shoulder, or even the leg in real defense, in the event that you are sitting or kneeling. What is important for nomenclature is only the angle, not the target.

11.1.3. TECHNIQUES FOR THE ADVANCED

Once again we go back to our simple application. Attack no. 1 is made and you have answered with no. 4. This second cut toward the arm ought to stop the attacker. However, in general it is not recommended to act on the attacker's inside (between both arms) and in reach of the other extremities. To come to the outside as quickly as possible, guide your knife underneath the attacker's weapon arm and press his arm upward with your wrist.

As soon as the blade can take over this task, allow it. It is always safer and easier to use the tool. Now the knife controls the weapon arm, and your free hand can push toward the face. You can also disarm the attacker with your knife (e.g., by a cut at the thumb).

You see that from a piece of module 1-4-12 there arises an entire defense combination that follows the learned principles.

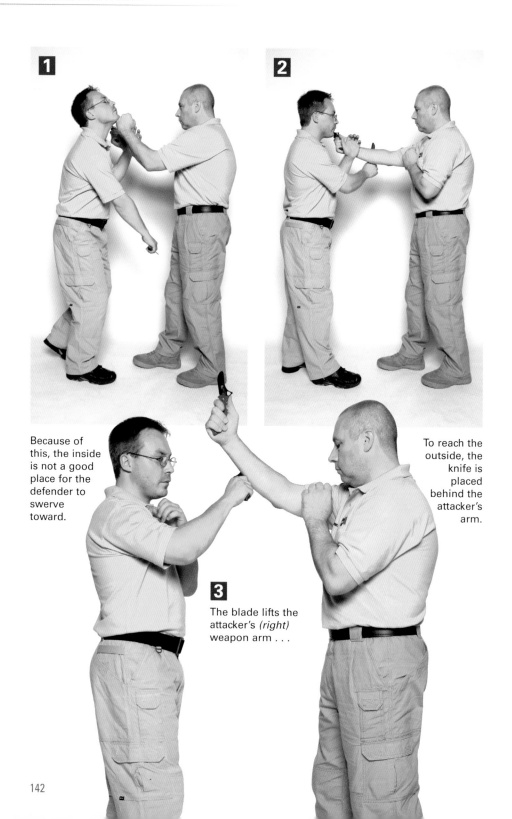

1

2

Because of this, the inside is not a good place for the defender to swerve toward.

To reach the outside, the knife is placed behind the attacker's arm.

3

The blade lifts the attacker's *(right)* weapon arm . . .

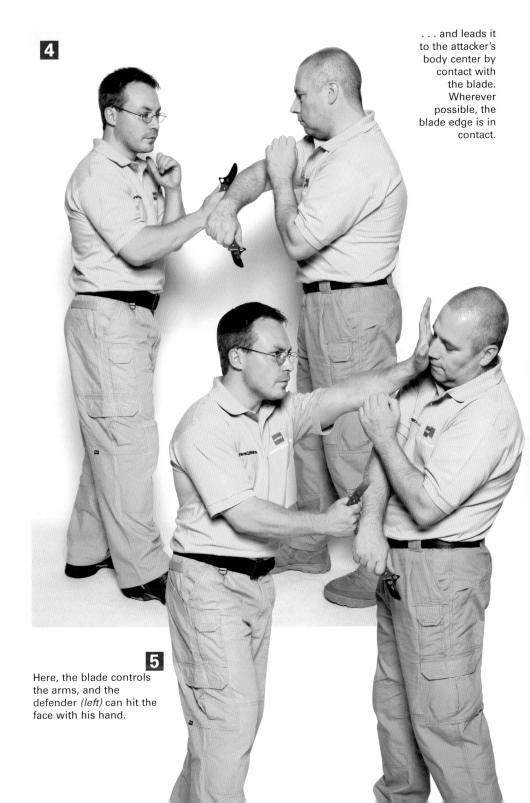

4

. . . and leads it to the attacker's body center by contact with the blade. Wherever possible, the blade edge is in contact.

5

Here, the blade controls the arms, and the defender *(left)* can hit the face with his hand.

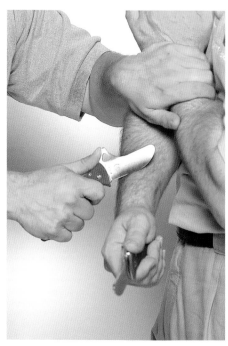

The free hand takes over control of the arms.

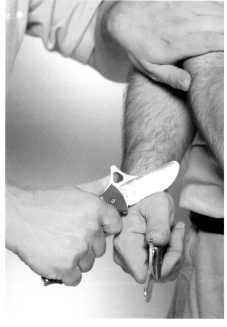

Disarming by cutting the thumb

The main thing is this: the connection 1-4 is not split up! Upon attack no. 1, defense with counterattack no. 4 thus always follows. This results logically from body position, mechanics, and situation in space.

The defense is made reflexively, without thinking, and thus creates a time frame within which you can add further actions, depending on need. If the attack is fended off for the time being and you have opened a window for further actions, you have all options and levels of escalation at your disposal in order to react as required by the situation.

Real applications are deduced from the forms of training (modules), and these are broadened, if necessary. In following these principles, we can also fend off an attack no. 4, which is stopped with the left arm, as in the module, by blocking the entire area on the side of your body where the attack is supposed to hit. Because there can always be multiple attacks or reactions of the attacker with respect to your stop, immediately cut the thumb of the knife hand in order to impair the weapon arm in its function. What would then follow in the training module? Right, the no. 12. While in general defined as a vertical movement, it is not made toward the head, as in the module, but toward the attacker's arm or shoulder. You remember that ultimately the target of the attack is not the determining factor of this concept, but only the angle that the blade describes in space. The next thing is to gain distance away from the attacker, and in a very simple way: move farther behind the attacker and push him forward with all your force. And voilà, you can get yourself to safety.

The attacker *(right)* starts with no. 4 toward the belly.

The defender *(left)* stops the arm and cuts across the hand.

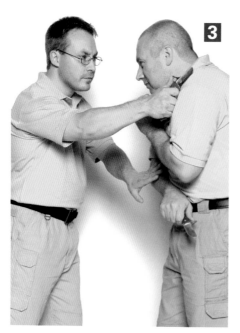

No. 12 here goes toward the shoulder on one side of the attacker . . .

. . . or toward the butt on the other side while running by at the same time. The cut in the hindquarters impairs the attacker's mobility.

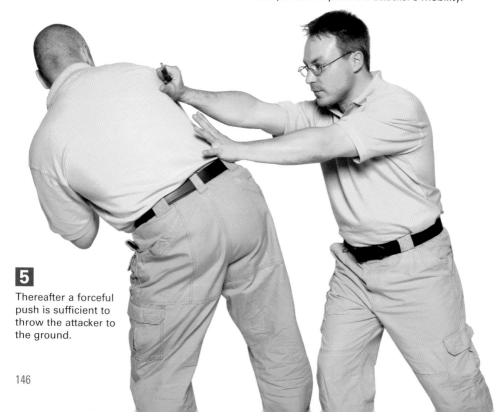

Thereafter a forceful push is sufficient to throw the attacker to the ground.

The no. 12 can be warded off as well: at first, the attack is stopped hard with your blade (the tip facing left), then you push the palm of your hand into the attacker's face, glide forward and to the right, and, while doing so, cut the attacking arm.

Since in the module a no. 1 follows the no. 12, you can perform this either on the attacking arm or the shoulder of the free hand, as you wish. If you want to reduce the attacker's mobility, the no. 1 can also be done toward the hip and thigh.

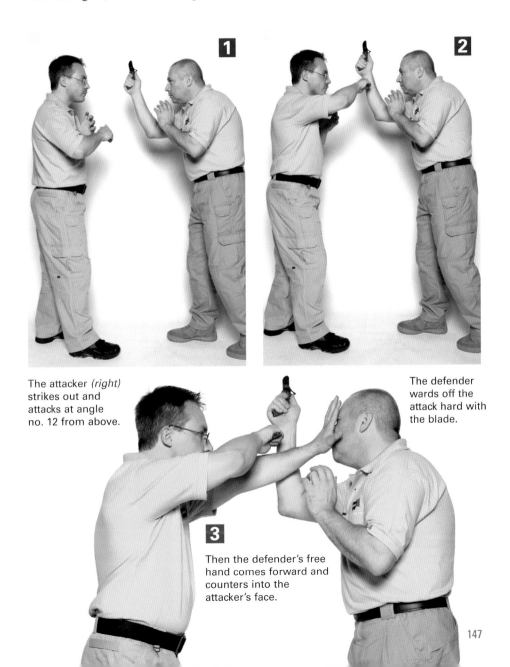

The attacker *(right)* strikes out and attacks at angle no. 12 from above.

The defender wards off the attack hard with the blade.

Then the defender's free hand comes forward and counters into the attacker's face.

Evading toward the side into the direction of one's own knife hand

Subsequent counterattack no. 1 toward the weapon hand

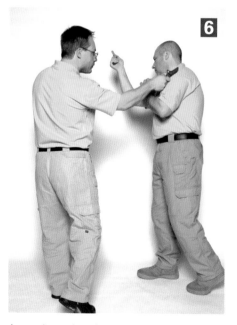

As an alternative, the counterattack at angle no. 1 is directed to the attacker's left shoulder.

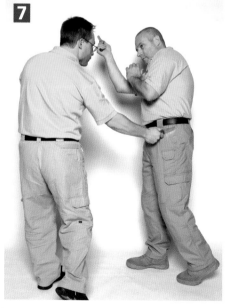

Or a cut toward the hip onset / thigh is made, which also approximates a no. 1.

I don't want to bring up the old discussion of whether or not you'll nearly always get injured yourself in an argument that involves knives. As is so often the case, the truth is probably somewhere in the middle. I can't imagine getting out of a confrontation with two blades whirring through the air without at least a scratch. On the other hand, I believe that it's really dangerous to just give in to fate and assume that you will be cut in any case.

Mental preparation is required not to get rigid from shock at the first cut. Whenever you injure yourself in training or make a mistake, or something doesn't work out the way you imagined, you have the chance to simulate an injury in reality. Don't simply stop and start the exercise from scratch again, but try under all circumstances to at least place one or two countercuts. Only then should you break contact with your partner and start anew. This way you learn to continue working in sudden situations and to not get scared stiff: don't automatically condition yourself to failure during training.

One way to prepare yourself for this eventuality is to also train your left hand. This way you can change the grip of your knife after sustaining cutting injuries to your right hand, or even draw a backup. It is important to be aware that you still have options with an injured right hand. Thus you can now work out module 1-4-12 backward with me. For this, we go back to the module's training form. Keep in mind that the roles of attacker and defender constantly change.

11.1.4. MODULE 1-4-12 (BACKWARD)

Attack no. 1 of your partner follows as before. According to the principle of "first the knife, then the hand," here, too, you block the at-

Partner *A (right)* attacks at an angle no. 1 toward the neck. He holds the knife in his right hand. Partner *B (left)* holds the knife with his left.

B stops the attack hard with his blade.

Then *A*'s arm is checked with the right (free) hand.

A counterattack with no. 4 follows.

tacking arm with the knife in the left hand. Cut toward your left hip and put the knife back by your right hand (cut and check).

Here you initially opened your arms; now you should close them again. Make a horizontal cut toward your partner's belly. Beware! Again, this is an exercise, not the real thing; otherwise we wouldn't cut the belly. Even though cut no. 4 was done with the left hand, it follows the same path as if done with the right hand.

Your partner stops with the free hand and cuts in the area of your thumb. Then he attacks you with no. 12, targeted to your head.

Here, a detail is changed in comparison with the standard version, but the principle stays the same. The tip of your blade faces left, as before. Now lift the knife and stop the attack. You will realize that the blade is oriented the same way as before, although it is in your other hand. This means that it is not important whether you are left- or right-handed; the one and only important consideration is the blade's orientation.

Now get your free hand in between the blade and attacker and onto his or her weapon arm. Check his or her arm and take it downward along your blade (a so-called slant block). This way you create some space for attacks in the area of the attacker's head.

You fill this space by attacking with a no. 1, which now—because you are working with your left hand—turns into a backhand. Your partner performs the "cut and check" and attacks with a no. 4. Again, your free hand blocks and the cut with the knife hand follows; thereafter no. 12 is performed, aiming at the head.

Your partner performs an umbrella block (see photo 16), because he or she still works with the right hand.

A (right) stops angle no. 4.

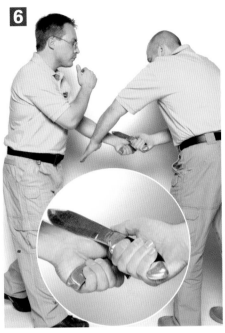

Then he cuts toward *B*'s weapon hand.

A's actual counterattack is performed as a no. 12 from above.

Angle no. 12 from above is stopped by a slant block. For this, *B* simply lifts his blade, similar to an "uppercut" in boxing.

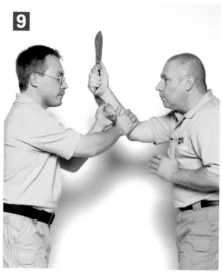

The umbrella block of module 1-4-12 (standard) from above now becomes a slant block. *B*'s free right hand moves in front of his own knife toward *A*'s arm and pulls it down.

By doing this, *A*'s arm is pulled downward and over *B*'s blade.

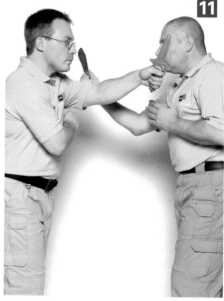

Now *B* (*left*) can start an attack at angle no. 1.

For *A*, nothing has changed in comparison with 1-4-12 (standard). He stops with his blade.

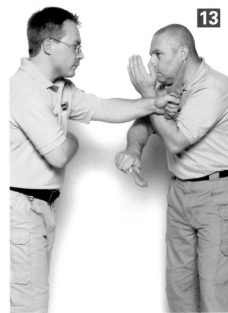

Then he checks *B*'s arm with his free left hand.

A counterattacks with no. 4.

B (*left*) stops and cuts across *A*'s weapon arm.

B (left) now counterattacks with no. 12.

A (right) stops and performs an umbrella block as before.

This ends the drill, and *A (right)* can now start with no. 1 again.

11.1.5. UMBRELLA BLOCK AND SLANT BLOCK

You will have recognized that there was a small change in warding off attack no. 12. Since no. 12 is performed vertically, you have basically two options for responding to it:

The umbrella block, as in the standard module, is used whenever your arms are closed and you have to open them. In addition, it allows evading in the direction of the hand holding a weapon. In contrast, the slant block, as in the backward mode, is used when your arms are open and have to be closed. In addition, you move in the direction of your free hand.

With the presentation of this information, all criteria that lead to a decision for one or the other kind of blocking are now described. In written form, of course, this sounds very theoretical. But you will see that by practicing the module in all its perspectives, a reflexive response will be quickly formed. Both methods of defense against an attack no. 12 (umbrella block as well as slant block) are performed with the right hand as weapon hand, although until now you have practiced the slant block only with your left hand. But this will change in the next section. Nevertheless, you can well recognize both options in defending against a no. 12.

1

2
Opening the arms for defense with an umbrella block

Attack with no. 12 from above. The defender's arms *(left)* are closed.

The defender *(left)* prepares the counterattack with no. 1.

Here, the slant block against no. 12: the open arms are now closed.

Preparing the counterattack with no. 2

11.2. MODULE 2-3-12: "THE OTHER SIDE"

The targets of angles 1, 4, and 12 form only part of the usual attacks. Still missing is the mirror-inverted image, but module 2-3-12 fills these gaps. This way, attacks with the high backhand and low forehand are covered as well. Again, practice this new module slowly at first with a partner and pay attention to exact performance.

11.2.1. MODULE 2-3-12 (STANDARD)

The attack starts with a no. 2 (a backhand) toward the right side of your neck. In the same way you fended off an attack to your left hand with "cut and check,"

you fend off this attack. But don't press the arm downward. Cut the weapon arm instead and take the knife to your right hip as in 1-4.

You opened your arms and now you close them again. This is done by means of an attack no. 3 toward the belly of your partner. He or she moves away from the weapon arm and stops the attack with the free hand, cuts the arm, and then, in turn, attacks with a no. 12 toward the head.

The following you already know from module "1-4-12 backward." You stop attack no. 12 with a slant block. Your free hand guides the attacker's weapon arm—located in front of your knife hand—along your blade. Your arms close, and this way you are ready for the backhand (attack no. 2).

A *(right)* starts with angle no. 2 toward B's neck *(left)*.

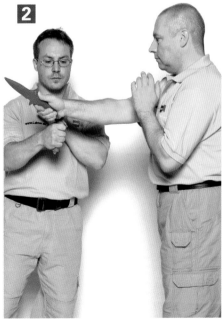

B stops with his blade.

Then *B* checks with his free hand.

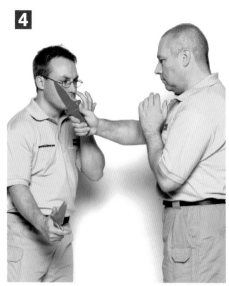

Thereafter, *B (left)* performs a counterattack no. 3 toward *A*'s belly.

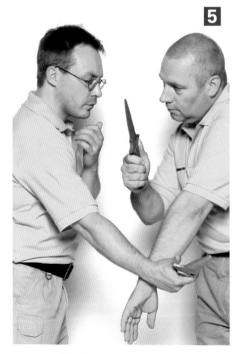

A stops with his free hand . . .

. . . and cuts across *B*'s weapon hand.

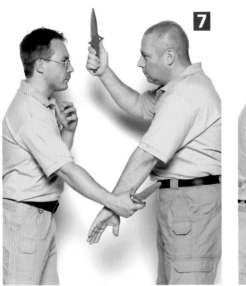

A now counterattacks with no. 12.

B stops hard with a slant block . . .

. . . and then leads A's
arm downward.

Now *B* can start the second half of the drill with no. 2.

A (right) now has to stop and check.

A (right) performs attack no. 3.

B stops with his free hand . . .

. . . and cuts *A*'s weapon hand.

Then angle no. 12 by *B* follows.

A performs a slant block . . .

. . . and counterattacks with no. 2, which marks a new beginning of the drill.

You will see that once you have mastered module 1-4-12, the other side with module 2-3-12 doesn't pose a big problem. The applications for a real defense here, too, are a logical result of the module sequence.

11.2.2. USES OF 2-3-12

An attacker tries to hit you at the neck with a no. 2 and to cut you there. Even though cut no. 2 is almost a stab, for the defender nothing changes because your position in relation to the attacking arm is decisive.

But this time the attack on you comes from the right. As you already learned in the previous module 1-4-12, you stop the attack with the knife, cut the arm, and check with your hand. As you have trained in module 2-3-12, you now perform cut no. 3.

In a real situation, a belly cut here would probably have lethal consequences for the attacker but would not stop him or her immediately. It is more reasonable to apply the cut a bit lower and to cut the thigh. Another effective possibility to impair the mobility of your opponent is to sever the connection between hip and thigh with the no. 3.

The principle of movements of the training form is followed, but its use is oriented toward real effectiveness as well as legal and social conventions.

The attacker *(right)* moves with a cut no. 2 toward the neck.

The defender *(left)* stops with his blade, . . .

. . . cuts the attacking arm, and checks.

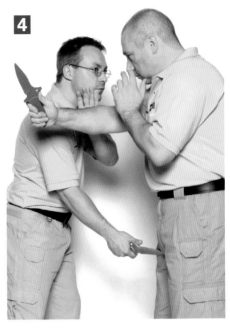

Counterattack no. 3 is performed lower than in the module and is directed toward the leg.

As an alternative, you can also cut toward the other leg.

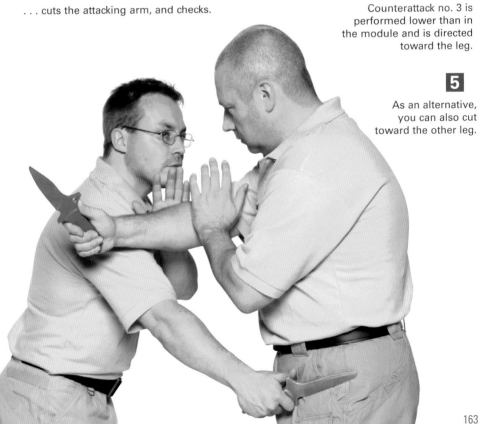

Whatever you decide on, the cutting angle you need for this is best achieved by using attack no. 3. Maneuver yourself behind the attacker and kick the hollow of his or her knee with your right foot. This way you will fell your opponent and can rescue yourself from this life-threatening situation.

From the training form, all other uses for the following angles can be deduced without any problems. The attacker tries to hit your belly with a cut no. 3. You stop the attack with your left arm and immediately cut the inside of the weapon arm. With this you gain a fraction of a second.

According to the module, a no. 12 follows now, which, for example, you can place on the upper arm. Here, the biceps tendon connecting upper arm and forearm is an excellent target. Severing it leads to overstretching the arm, which then can easily be levered or broken. As always, at this point you can also simply flee.

The defender positions himself behind the attacker and takes him to the ground by a kick to the hollow of the knee.

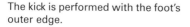

The kick is performed with the foot's outer edge.

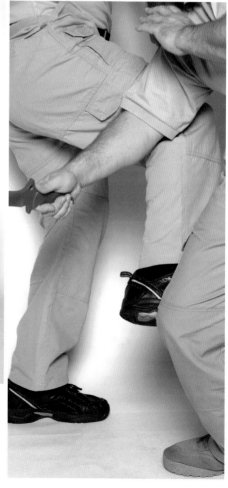

The attacker *(left)* attacks with no. 3 toward the defender's belly.

The defender stops with his free hand and cuts the attacking arm.

Then follows counterattack no. 12 toward the weapon arm at the biceps.

11.2.3. DEFENSE IN REVERSE GRIP

For better understanding, here you can look at training form 1-4-12 in reverse grip. In the reverse grip, the defense doesn't behave differently from that in forward grip. The blade still follows the same path in space. Ultimately it doesn't matter whether a stab or cut is performed, but for practicing the modules you always ought to stick to cutting, because this way the parallels to the forward grip can be understood most easily. Just imagine that the knife would fly through the air by itself and keep its orientation as if guided by a ghost's hand.

It doesn't matter how you place your hand on the knife. If the tip of the knife blade faces left in forward grip, it does the same in reverse grip. If the blade moves from the right to the left in forward grip, it will move in space in the same way with the reverse grip.

A (right) cuts an angle no. 1 in reverse grip toward *B*'s neck.

B stops the attack with his blade, which here is oriented in the same way as in the forward grip previously.

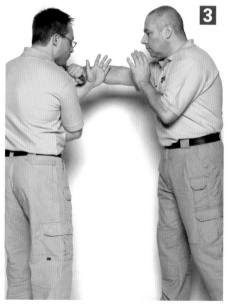

After the cut follows a check with the free hand.

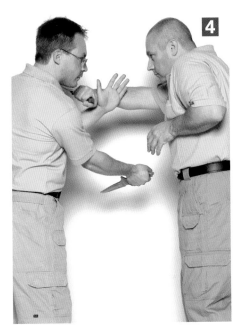

B (left) performs a no. 4.

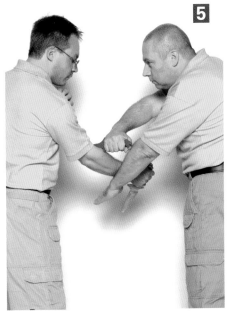

A stops with his free hand and cuts the weapon arm *(crosswise here)*.

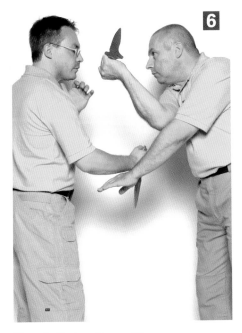

Then *A* attacks with no. 12.

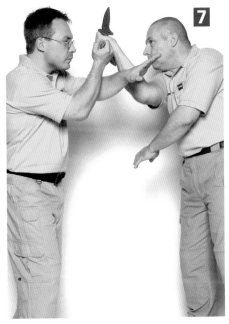

B lifts the blade without changing the tip's orientation and performs an umbrella block.

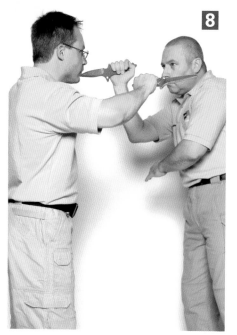

Then *B* is able to attack with no. 1.

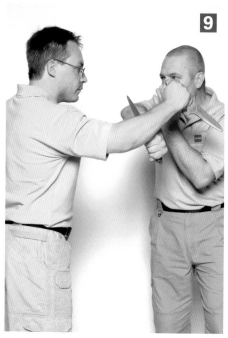

A stops with his blade, checks, . . .

. . . and counterattacks with no. 4.

B stops with his free arm . . .

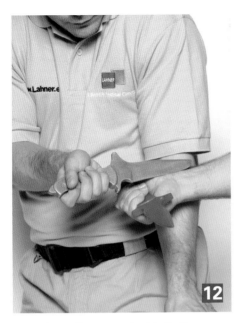

. . . and cuts (here seen in detail) *A*'s weapon hand, with *B*'s blade oriented the same way as in the forward grip.

Then follows a no. 12 by *B*.

A stops the blade with an umbrella block.

Then *A* can start the drill again from the beginning.

With this description, it ought to be possible for you to practice module 2-3-12 in reverse grip too. Now you can easily deduce the principles you have to use in the following applications. Please keep in mind that both opponents in the photo stand close to each other. But in reality, if possible, you should choose a distinctly greater distance.

The attacker stands before you threateningly, and your left hand is raised for an appeasing gesture while you cover your knife with the right hand in reverse grip. Since your arms are open, you have to ward off the oncoming attack with a slant block. By turning your wrist you orient your blade anew and then cut the attacker's shoulder muscles. This way you impede the attacker from lifting his arm in a bio-mechanical way. Because your arms are now open, you can close them again and thus place a second counterattack at the weapon arm.

1

The attacker *(right)* threatens. The defender *(left)* hides his knife behind his leg so as not to escalate the situation himself.

2

The attacker stabs toward the face.

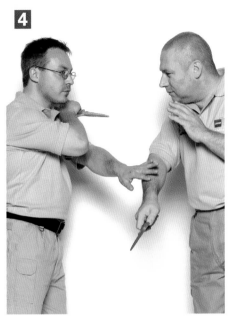

The defender treats this as an attack no. 12 and performs a slant block.

The defender prepares himself for a counterattack no. 2.

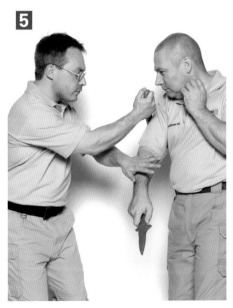

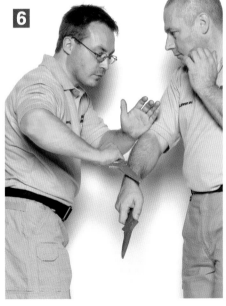

This is performed across the shoulder muscles . . .

. . . and, if necessary, back across the inside of the attacking weapon arm.

11.3. MODULE 1-2-2

This module, also called "high-line drill," doesn't cover any new angles. Nevertheless, it is very important because in the counterattack it is instead oriented upward, not downward. In addition, it functions as a connective element between the other modules and enables a seamless change.

In modules 1-4-12 and 2-3-12, after the attack with no. 1 or 2, you always oriented yourself downward in the form of a no. 3 or 4 for the counterattack. By "downward" I mean the area from the elbow down. This is also called "low line." In general, every attack has the possibility of being high or low, and your counterattack can be high or low in the same way.

In module 1-4-12, after attack no. 1, a no. 4 follows as a counterattack. The background is that during a clash of two opponents, usually there is no space left between their bodies. If you cut downward against the attacking arm, it is usually not possible to make a counterattack upward to the shoulder area. Either the opponent's arm or your own is in the way. Instead there is a gap in the low line, which can be used in the form of a no. 4.

There are situations in which the counterattack has to be placed differently. If, for example, the attacker is protected by gear or protective clothing, you perhaps will have to work upward.

It can also happen that a no. 1 as an attack is performed almost straight, like a stab, and you hardly have enough time to take your knife to your opponent's weapon arm. Often there is not enough space to place the check hand between the knife and your head, which means that you can reach with your free hand only from underneath your weapon arm. Here, too, module 1-2-2 comes into play. In addition, the high-line drill offers further options for the well-known angles.

When training with your partner, you can begin with 1-4-12 and then seamlessly combine all attacks and counterattacks by means of 1-2-2. This way you advance slowly and step by step from module to module and will be able to quickly turn to free sparring.

And this is how module 1-2-2 works: you are attacked by your partner with a no. 1. This time he is stabbing toward your face. On the one hand, you thereby learn a defense against stabs, and on the other hand your partner's attack helps you with the correct performance of your defense. You "fetch the attacker's arm with the knife from behind" and guide it forward and to the side. Here, a turn of your body for evasion is especially important.

A (left) attacks with a stab no. 1.

When the knife has almost arrived at your shoulder, move your free hand under and beyond your weapon arm to check your opponent's weapon arm. Your arms are now closed.

Now the roles are switched. As an attacker, you open your arms and execute a no. 2 (high line) toward your partner's neck. He or she first checks with the left hand, because the knife hand is not within reach. Your partner closes his or her arms and cuts as with the slant block.

Important: your partner's free hand has to be placed in front of his knife. This way he can check your weapon hand downward while still working high (high line) without blocking himself.

Now the way is free for him to start an attack no. 2 of his own. You check it with your free hand and, by turning your body, move your knife to the upper right to cut your partner's weapon arm. This sequence unfolds especially if your weapon arm is still controlled by your partner. By the rotation of your body, your controlled hand is freed again.

If your partner is not in control anymore, the knife can stop the attack first, then the hand checks. Now cut downward, then "weasel" an attack no. 1 around your partner's weapon arm as an attack toward his face. I say "weasel" because, with the knife suddenly appearing in front of his face, you compel him to do this exercise correctly. He should react with the knife in a panic, so that his free hand doesn't get around to check.

B parries the stab and guides it to his left side with his knife.

B's free hand moves to the front under his own weapon hand and checks.

173

Now *B* counterattacks with no. 2.

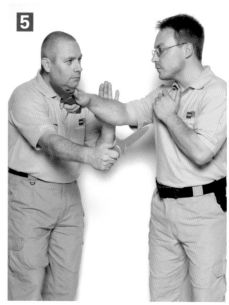

A stops with his free hand . . .

. . . and then cuts in combination with a slant block.

Thereafter, *A* counterattacks with no. 2.

B stops with his free hand . . .

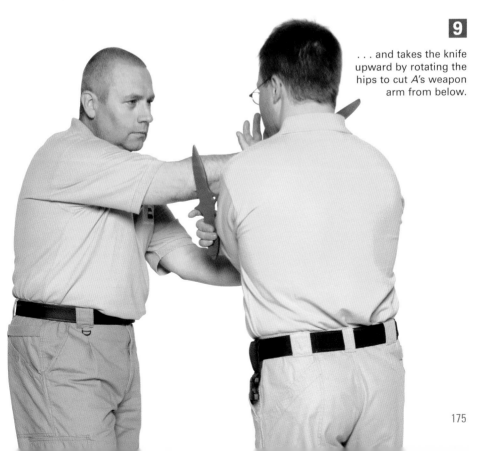

. . . and takes the knife upward by rotating the hips to cut *A*'s weapon arm from below.

From there, *B* now too attacks with a no. 1 as a stab.

A (*left*) guides *B*'s stab past him . . .

. . . and checks with his left. From there he is able to continue with a no. 2.

11.4. PEN AGAINST KNIFE

The movements with the knife can be transferred to everyday utensils. This is an especially interesting aspect of the Modular System. In contrast to knives, everyday items are available everywhere and can be carried unobtrusively. Even in situations in which you are occupied with other things and when an attack by surprise, you may have a ballpoint pen, a key, newspapers, a book, or something similar at hand. Just imagine your ballpoint pen as a knife and practice the following situation:

While the defender (a police officer in our example) is still taking notes, his opponent suddenly draws a knife and tries to stab him. The defender draws the tip of the ballpoint pen across the attacker's weapon arm while holding the arm with his free hand. Subsequently there follows a forceful stab into the shoulder muscles with the backhand and another one to the chest with the forehand.

Since for police officers in such a case the goal is not escape but arrest, the takedown is performed starting from a closed position. The left hand pushes the attacker's upper torso backward while the right hand rams the ballpoint pen into the attacker's chest/shoulder and pulls forward. From there, an arrest can be made.

The police officer *(left)* jots down data.

Suddenly the attacker *(at right)* stabs toward his face. The officer drops the pad and uses the pen as a weapon in reverse grip.

3

The pen slows down the attack; its tip rips across the lower arm while the free hand checks.

4

The officer hammers on the weapon arm with his pen while controlling with his left arm at the same time.

5

Further hits with the pen on the muscles of the weapon arm follow. Depending on the situation, these can also be placed onto the attacker's face.

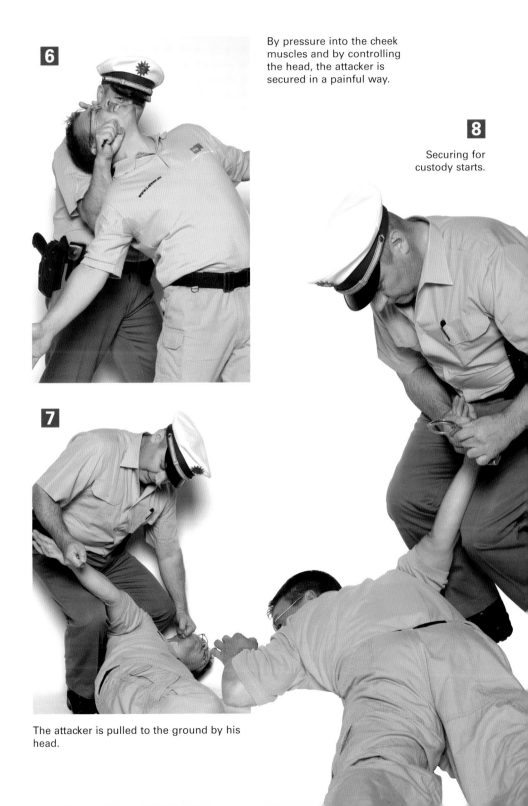

6

By pressure into the cheek muscles and by controlling the head, the attacker is secured in a painful way.

8

Securing for custody starts.

7

The attacker is pulled to the ground by his head.

11.5. WEAPON RETENTION

For people carrying firearms, the use of the Modular System for preventing their weapons from being wrested from them is especially interesting. Despite the advent of modern holsters, you should not rely too much on the integrated safeties, because during a fight there is enough pushing, pulling, and getting jammed to unlock these. Frequently the "arm wrap" with "horizontal elbow" is taught for weapon retention (securing one's own weapon). The risk of the attacker staggering after a hit with the elbow is quite high. Since the attacker is quite often taller and heavier than the defender, in falling he pulls the defender down while wresting the weapon away from him. Both possibly end up in a ground fight situation, which has become even more dangerous because of the weapon.

In our example, you see a guard at a checkpoint. During the check of papers, an attacker suddenly reaches for the guard's weapon. The grip brings attacker and defender into the same position as with an attack no. 4. The reaction in principle is also the same as with a no. 4, but it makes sense to retain the defender's hand at the weapon to suppress further pulling. Thus, only the left hand remains free. With this, the guard reaches for his knife and cuts the attacker's arm, as we did with 1-4-12 backward. As a result, the grip on the weapon gets loosened considerably or is detached completely.

With the knife in reverse grip, the attacking arm is led to the outside; the free hand still secures the weapon. A cut toward the leg on the way back enables the creation of distance, which can't be compensated for by the attacker because of his lack of mobility. While still keeping the knife in hand, the guard brings his primary weapon into aiming position. Drawing his handgun would be possible. But since drawing the handgun from the holster amid the pushing and pulling is not safe, the soldier decides on his primary weapon. He may shoot or start the arrest.

The attacker *(left)* comes close to the guard.

He is reaching for the weapon:

Instead of working with his physical strength, the guard secures his weapon with one hand while drawing the knife with the other.

In a continuation of the drawing process, he cuts both arms of the attacker from left to right.

By "hooking," he takes the attacker's arms out of the way and to the left . . .

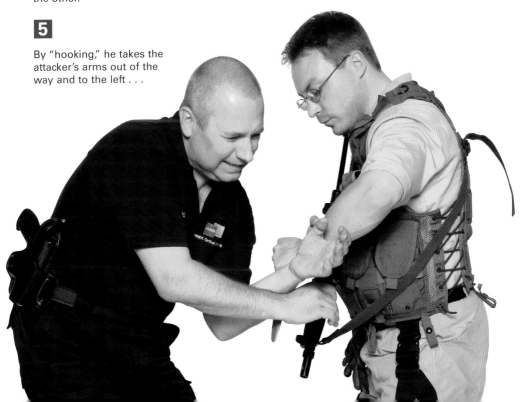

6

. . . and cuts the attacker's leg.

7

The attacker is injured; the guard creates some distance.

8

With the knife still in his hand, the guard deploys his firearm.

11.6. APPLICATION WITH EMPTY HANDS

In the modules of the Modular System, not only weapon techniques are taught. In the next example you'll see how a knife attack can be initially fended off with empty hands before one's own tool is drawn. The key to success is to imagine your own hand as a knife.

As soon as the defender grabs, blocks hard, or keeps at the opponent's weapon arm for too long, he himself will inevitably be cut. Thus it is necessary to look at one's hand as a knife. If, in the flow of actions, this is used in a quick and cutting way, keeping up with the dynamics of a blade confrontation is enabled far better.

Of course, the topmost priority is to bring your own tool into play as quickly as possible. But if you put too much attention on drawing the weapon and don't focus on the defense, you may have to pay dearly for it. This, for example, can often be seen with people carrying firearms.

In order to draw one's own weapon, at least one of the following points has to be fulfilled:

The opponent's hand closest to your own weapon has to be controlled.

There has to be a sufficient distance for giving you enough time to draw the weapon before the attacker can make contact again.

The opponent should be under pressure from kicks or hits.

The opponent should be in such a movement away from the defender that he can hardly turn around in time to suppress the process of drawing the weapon.

In our example the attacker stabs out of nowhere toward the face of the defender. Only by a quick turn of the body and by guiding the weapon arm past with the right hand can the defender avoid the stab. Here,

the right hand is used instead of a knife as in module 1-2-2. If your hand is not kept stiff in certain positions but keeps in motion all the time, certain chances arise.

The defender's check hand now alternates in contact with the "weapon hand" in order to keep each hand at the weapon arm for as short a time as possible. This way the risk of being cut by a withdrawal movement is minimized.

A push with the ball of the weapon hand toward the attacker's face or a stab into the eyes follows immediately. Here you have to react within a fraction of a second, depending on whether there is an

1

The attacker *(left)* stabs toward the guard's face.

effect on the attacker or not. If there is an effect, you continue.

If your defense doesn't show any effects, then you don't have any protection from further attacks of your opponent. Thus you must create some distance, and in any case don't try to grab the moving knife in order to control the arm. You won't succeed in this without previous strong hits. The whole action basically is similar to that of a boxer who always judges whether he can take the risk to start the infighting now.

We assume you hit. Then a second push with the free hand follows. Here, the

defender moves away from the attacker's weapon arm. The left hand stays in front and pushes the attacker in the face as forcefully as possible. The momentum is kept and the attacker is downright overrun. He is not allowed to find a solid base anymore but ought to actually wobble or stagger in front of the defender.

At the same time the defender's right hand grasps his or her own weapon and draws it. Now the attacker's legs can be cut (angle nos. 1 and 2, or 3 and 4 alternating). This way a safe escape is possible. But the last cuts are justified only in the event that the attacker still poses a threat.

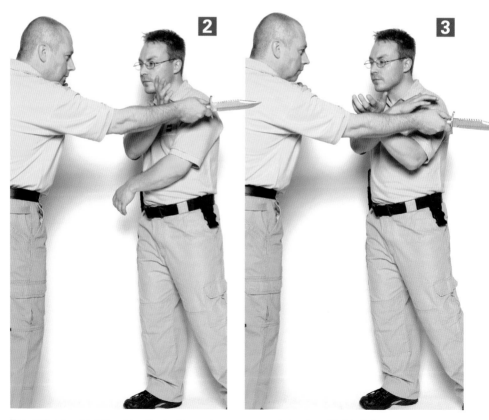

The defender *(right)* guides the knife past himself as in module 1-2-2 . . .

. . . and checks with his left.

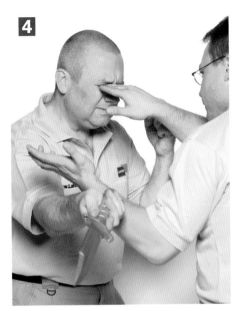

Counterattack no. 2 here follows as a quick stab toward the eyes.

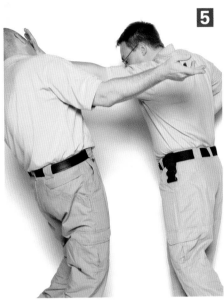

The following heavy blow toward the face with the left hand and drawing the knife with the right are performed at the same time.

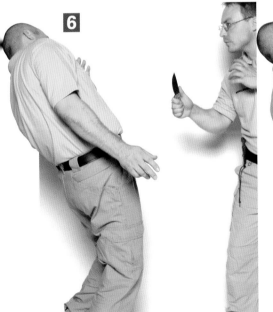

The knife is drawn and ready for use.

If necessary, the attacker's mobility can be impaired by cuts toward the leg.

11.7. ATTACK NO. 5: THE GOLDEN MEAN

You probably have been asking yourself for some time already about where's the infamous stab toward the belly. It's simple: you have already been able to defend yourself against this for quite a while. Stab no. 5 is nothing else but the radius of a circle. The circle is created when you cut at angles nos. 3 and 4. Any stab on this circular area is a no. 5 and can be warded off the same as a no. 3 or 4.

Depending on where you stand, you thus parry the no. 5 with your free hand toward the outside or inside, then cut across the attacker's weapon arm—just as you learned in modules 1-4-12 and 2-3-12. In the end this depends on which direction you evade toward and on which side of your body the attacking arm ends up after the movement. And you have to evade, because this will give you the decisive security of not staying in the opponent's line of attack. Your check hand helps you only a little bit in this.

The attacker *(at right)* stabs straight toward the body's center with a no. 5. The defender *(left)* evades toward the left and secures the attacking arm with his free arm. Now the cut to the weapon hand can be performed, as learned by defending against no. 4.

In this image the no. 5 is led toward the other side and treated as a no. 3.

11.7.1. DEFENSE AGAINST A STAB TOWARD THE ABDOMEN WITH CHECK AND CUT

The attacker stabs toward the body's center. Because the defender would be hit a bit outside the center, he decides on evading toward the left. The defender leads his attack with the free hand toward the right and treats it like an attack no. 4. For this, he steps back with his right leg and turns his body away. A cut toward the attacker's weapon hand follows immediately to keep it away from the defender's body and to impair its function.

According to module 1-4-12, after attack no. 4 there follows a counterattack toward the attacker's upper arm by means of the no. 12. Since the arms are closed, the opening movement can be combined with another no. 4 toward the attacker's arm.

The attacker *(right)* stabs with no. 5. The defender *(left)* checks as if against no. 4.

Then follows a cut toward the weapon hand, as in module 1-4-12, . . .

. . . and a counterattack no. 12 toward the attacker's upper arm.

11.7.2. DEFENSE AGAINST A STAB TOWARD THE ABDOMEN WITH CUT AND CHECK

In the previous example the defense followed the principle of "check and cut." I chose this for the example because it exactly matches the approach and course of action in the module. But as you know, there are good reasons, if at all possible, to first use the tool against the weapon arm and only then against the hand (cut and check). This way you are less endangered of being injured and you create an immediate reaction by the attacker after the very first contact.

There is nothing against first using the knife against nos. 3, 4, and 5 and using the hand only thereafter. The prerequisite for this is for the tool to be quickest to reach the attacker's weapon arm. Thus, here is the same example of a defense, but this time with cut and check.

The attacker stabs with a no. 5 toward the belly. The defender turns away from the line of attack and to the right, and this time fends off the attack with the knife first. Then he moves the knife upward in order to cut the weapon hand. Then he returns the knife to by his free arm to sustain protection of his body while preparing the counterattack. As before, this is performed with a no. 12 and a no. 4.

The defender *(left)* deflects the attack no. 5 to the side with his blade.

His free hand checks after the knife has been cutting upward.

From there, a cut
to the shoulder
follows, . . .

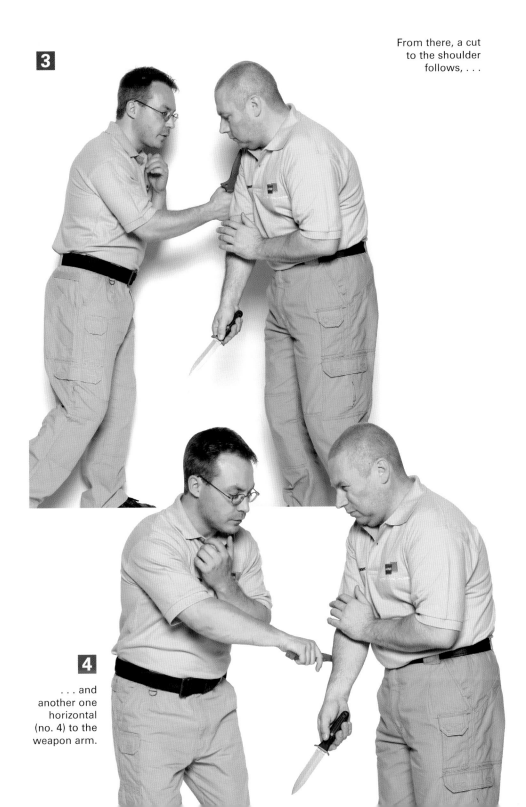

3

4

. . . and
another one
horizontal
(no. 4) to the
weapon arm.

11.8. DEFENSE WITH A STICK

The stick as a means of defense offers a multitude of options and can cover a broad spectrum of escalation levels. Among others, material and construction type are important for operational success. Internationally, a distinctive trend away from special sticks (such as the variants of the tonfa) becomes apparent. The reason for this derives from the experience that the training effort for achieving good results is disproportionately higher. In addition, if you watch tonfa users under stress, in the end you see them grabbing the tonfa as if it were a normal stick and then hitting.

With the introduction of better and better materials and especially locking mechanisms too, more and more good arguments speak in favor of expandable batons. I want to remark here that in Germany, according to the new weapons law, carrying these is not allowed anymore for civilians. However, several models are available for the government sector.

In the event that the lock works with friction, the user forgoes an important advantage of the stick: an excellent expandable baton with sufficient mass and very good lock, such as, for example, the EKA of the company Bonowi, can be opened and closed during the course of a confrontation. This can be done in an unobtrusive and de-escalating way, or aggressively. But mainly you are able to work with the closed baton in a confined space and open it in the course of the fight, if necessary.

But I have to warn you of a false assessment: a stick is always a bad choice against knives and blades,

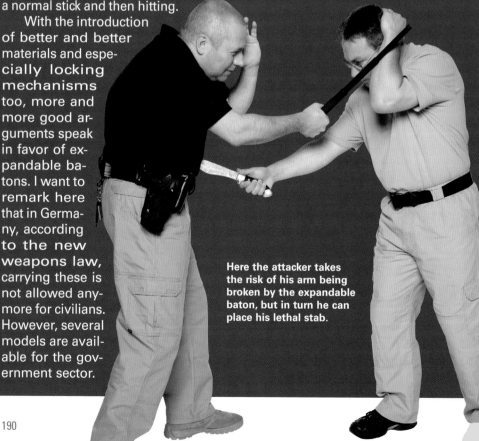

Here the attacker takes the risk of his arm being broken by the expandable baton, but in turn he can place his lethal stab.

because an advantage in reach will always be canceled out by a determined opponent. And to hit a moving hand, to knock the knife out of an opponent's hand, is anything but easy.

However, the expandable baton is very effective against impact weapons. In this case, the advantage of long reach really matters, and, with well-placed hits, a good stick can have a severe effect even on large groups of muscles. And the Modular System works with the stick as well.

The attacker takes aim with the bottle.

1

Hit no. 1 is stopped by a counterhit with the stick on the attacking arm.

2

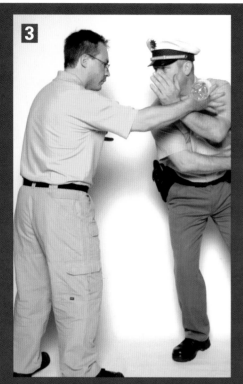

The hit is carried out and the free hand briefly secures the attacking arm.

The attacker's weapon drops and a hit toward the leg follows as a counterattack.

5

The stick goes over the shoulder to the attacker's neck, is grabbed with both hands, and is pulled toward the defender. Thus the attacker can be taken down in a controlled way.

The attacker grabs the police officer's weapon arm.

The officer evades sideways, takes the unextended stick over the attacker's wrist, and can then give the elbow a blow with the free hand.

. . . and checking over the neck and pulling backward may follow.

The stick is extended by its momentum, . . .

Although I already pointed out the risks of defending with a stick against knives, there are nevertheless situations in which it is the only available means of defense. In our next example the employee of a security company, standing in front of a nightclub, is molested. Calmly and politely he banishes the uninvited guest from the club. Because the uninvited guest now threatens to "pay him back and do him in," the security professional, for protection, opens the expandable baton behind his back but nevertheless stays polite. The uninvited guest appears to back off but then turns and stabs with no. 5. The defender hits hard against the attacker's arm to deflect the stab; all his force has to be put into this hit. This is the decisive factor for not getting hit. At the same time, a movement out of the line of attack has to be performed. The defender's free hand secures the free space to protect the belly from possible cuts and to achieve a temporary control of the weapon arm. The no. 12 (now following in the module) is executed forcefully onto the attacker's hand, thus removing the knife. By a combined control of the neck and destabilization (direction of pull to the back and downward) the attacker can be brought down or controlled.

1

The employee of a security company *(left)* tries to calm down the uninvited guest, who is already hiding a knife behind his leg.

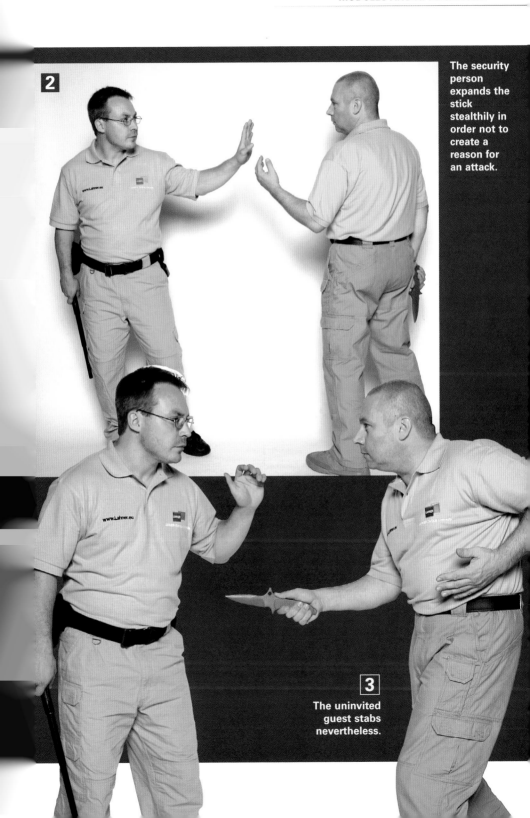

2

The security person expands the stick stealthily in order not to create a reason for an attack.

3

The uninvited guest stabs nevertheless.

By a blow with the stick and evasion, the defender takes the knife out of the line of attack.

The free arm secures briefly, and as much space as possible is used for gathering momentum.

6

The blow to the weapon arm leads to dropping the knife.

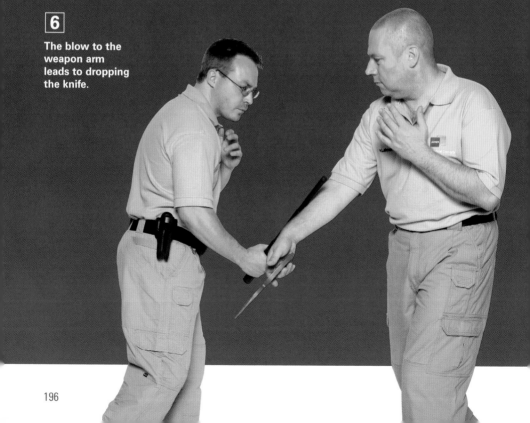

7

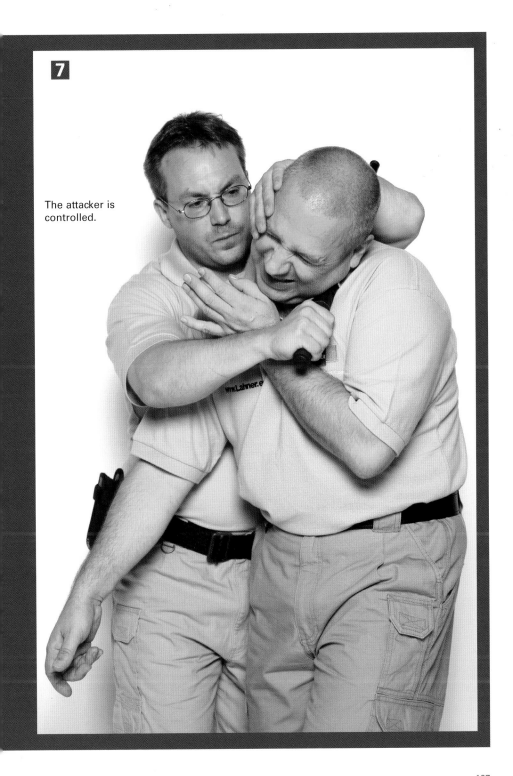

The attacker is controlled.

CHAPTER TWELVE

DEFENSE AGAINST KNIVES AND BLADES

A book about self-defense with the knife would not be complete without discussing the difficulties in fending off knives and blades, at least at an elementary level. Right away it has to be said that this topic is one of the most controversial in the area of self-defense. One of the reasons for this is that edged weapons are the most dangerous instruments at close distance.

Therefore, a successful defense with bare hands against a knife is not completely impossible, but nevertheless very difficult. Now it doesn't exactly flatter the image of an effective fighting system if you have to admit that a large percentage of the attacks can't be fended off. Thus, in various self-defense systems the attacks are performed in ways that are often far from real-life situations, in order to be able to demonstrate very artistic-looking defense techniques that are not really effective.

Actual attacks with knives and blades are usually extremely fast and dynamic, chaotic, and violent. Usually there is not just a single attack, but a whole staccato of stabs and cuts. In contrast to the defense against hits and kicks, it is not sufficient to protect yourself provisionally and to hope for hits bouncing off the shielding arms or only touching the body lightly. While you may be able to handle one or the other hit or kick under stress while pumped up with adrenaline, any contact with the blade means extreme and potentially lethal injuries or loss of function of the extremities, which are important for defense.

And just here is the problem: Who can guarantee never to be hit, or just grazed? You have to be aware that a defense against blades in most cases also means getting injured.

This attitude is often criticized because it is said to weaken the will to fight. I regard this as wrong; I see this attitude only as being realistic. As a defender, you should not conjure up an injury, but you should be ready to work with it when it happens.

It is important to learn two things from this: first, you shouldn't train in practice to give up when any small injury or pain occurs, but you should fire at least one or two basic techniques against your attacking partner before interrupting the training to look at the injuries. Transferred into reality, this training attitude teaches fighting to the end, regardless of injuries or disturbing factors. The old proverb "you fight the way you train" is all too true.

Second, proceeding from the fact that an injury during the fight is very probable, you should under no circumstances conclude never to fight with empty hands against an edged weapon. As reasonable as this may sound, it is far removed from real practice. I think I have mentioned enough reasons why it makes sense to fend off an edged weapon with a tool. However, confrontations with edged weapons don't usually take place in the form of sportive competition or duels, but the attack takes place with the advantages on the attacker's side. This may be an ambush, a surprise attack, an attack on apparently uninvolved persons, or the defender's misinterpretation of the situation.

Something that all these possibilities have in common is that the defender can't draw his tool in time. Thus he or she first has to open a time slot with bare hands during which he or she can reach for their own tool. Until this time, the defense necessarily has to be performed with bare hands. If running off or de-escalation is not possible, this is the only option. In this case, no witty proverb such as "distance is your friend" is really helpful. Usually, you as a defender just don't determine the parameters of the confrontation.

How then to defend against a knife? Because in the end, it is you whose life is endangered in a situation such as this. It holds true that you should defend yourself by means of the techniques and concepts you feel sure about and, in a training situation, can apply under stress against a partner defending himself or herself successfully and reproducibly. If you can succeed eight out of ten times in fetching the blade with your teeth and disarming your opponent in this way, then you are better than anybody I have ever met. But if it works—congratulations! Use your ability!

Just don't let anybody talk you into believing that one or another technique is better than anything else. Learn them all, practice them, and test whether they function under conditions as close to reality as possible. The characteristics, body build, motor skills, and abilities of humans are too different to offer a universal solution to each situation. Thus I can only give you suggestions and tips that work for me and many of my students. This isn't the be-all and end-all either.

In real scenarios I have seen repeatedly that the defender is injured especially when he is behaving too statically. Attacks with knifes are so fast and dynamic that it is essential to behave in a similar way in order to keep up. A simple way to achieve this is to fight with empty hands in such a way as if you were holding a knife. This forces you to make fast, flowing, and dynamic movements and prevents static and staccato concepts.

In particular, professional users of firearms can't avoid practicing defense against a blade with empty hands, because their firearm often can't be drawn in time.

CHAPTER THIRTEEN

SUMMARY

The modules comprise training forms that prepare you for real applications. You ought to practice the modules time and again individually. While doing so, change the grip (forward and reverse) as well as the perspectives (standard, backward, mirror image, and backward-backward). Always use the blade first (training knife!), then figure out how other items can be fit into these concepts. The more you yourself experiment while doing so, the clearer the underlying principles become.

Even if you have fun with the movements, the rhythm, and the increase in your own abilities, don't forget one thing: these are just exercises on the way to learning real applications for your defense. The biggest mistake, unfortunately made by many, is to turn into a hunter and gatherer of drills and forms of training. Entire systems are based on the fact that a person wearing a black belt can recite two more forms of training by heart than a person wearing a brown belt. But this doesn't say anything about the ability to defend oneself.

The next step on the way to free defense is the ease with which you can flow from one situation into the next one. When you look more closely at the modules, you will realize that the possibility exists at several points to change from one module to another.

From attack no. 1 you can change to 1-4-12 (low line) or 1-2-2 (high line). There you have the possibility of continuing with 1-2-2 in high line following attack 2, or to

change to 2-3-12 (low line).

You can use a slant block as in module 1-2-2 against an attack no. 2 (your free hand is in front of your knife) and thus answer with a no. 2, or you can go deep

Starting position with attack no. 1 by *A (left)*. *B (right)* stops the attack with his blade.

and answer with a no. 4 (for this, the knife has to be in front of your free hand during the slant block). Instead of a no. 3 or 4, you can use a no. 5 at any time, because—as we now know—this is a radius on the same area of a circle. In reverse, you can treat attack no. 5 the same as a no. 3 or 4.

Approach gradually toward free training. For this, you best start with module 1-4-12 and count along. Now you change the sequence, but only at one position each time. For example, you can take up the

no. 1 and change to 1-2-2 high line. Stay at this for a while with your partner. At some point you decide to take out the no. 2 and replace it with a no. 3 low line to change into module 2-3-12. In the course of time you will be able to change more frequently and finally change attacks and counterattacks freely.

Below you can see with the example of 1-4-12 how you can answer the no. 1 either with a no. 4, thus staying with 1-4-12, or change to 1-2-2.

One possibility here consists of defending oneself according to module 1-4-12. *B* accordingly cuts downward . . .

. . . and counterattacks with no. 4, which can be stopped by *A*.

From the same starting situation after attack no. 1 by *A (left)*, module 1-2-2 can be accessed: after stopping the attack with the blade, the free arm comes forward underneath one's own knife and checks.

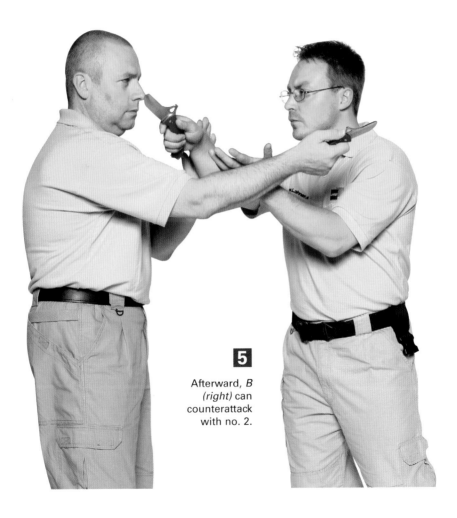

5

Afterward, *B*
(right) can
counterattack
with no. 2.

CHAPTER FOURTEEN
TRAINING AIDS FOR HOME

Many of my students and participants in seminars don't have the opportunity to train as often as they might want to. They live far away, some of them in foreign countries, and often they don't have a partner for training. However, there are a few simple options for training at home. These can't replace training with a partner defending himself or herself, but nevertheless you can enhance your abilities by means of them.

14.1. FOOTWORK

Movement is important. If you have the feeling of being too clumsy, then create a triangle on the ground and move as described in section 8.4, "Movements." In combination with music, you can also use this for working out.

14.2. DUMMY TRAINING

Most probably you don't have a Chinese wooden doll, but you can just get yourself two short sticks. You clamp these between the books in your bookshelf, about shoulder's width apart and at a bit higher level than your shoulders are. Now you already have a taller opponent in front of you who is attacking you with both arms.

Stand between both sticks and fend off the left stick first. Since this is an attack no. 1, this means that you should "cut, check, and counterattack with no. 4 toward the shelf." Immediately you turn toward

the right and ward off attack no. 2 of the other stick (with cut, check, and counterattack with no. 3). Here, you focus on the rotation of your hip and clean angles. You

Two sticks installed into book shelves—and you have an attacker willing to train.

also can clamp one of the sticks one board of the shelf higher up. The attack simulated in this way is warded off with an umbrella block and a slant block, alternately, and a counterattack with no. 1 or no. 2, respectively. The same stick a bit lower, at belly level, can be treated alternately with a no. 3 or 4.

Defense with cut and check against an imaginary no. 1.

You will see that this way you'll quickly start sweating and achieve a high number of repeats. You can screw the sticks securely in appropriate places, clamp them in, or even let somebody hold them. Be creative!

14.3. SHADOW "CUTTING"

Surely you know about shadow boxing. Well, in our case we just cut rather than box. Let yourself be attacked by imagined opponents and ward off all attacks by means of the Modular System. Here, too, don't forget that each attack in certain situations has only a limited number of reasonable counterattacks. This way you learn to move in a flowing style from one situation into the next one.

Even if a training partner is unable or unwilling to participate in the exercise, he or she is still able to hold the sticks, similar to training with focus mitts in boxing.

Here, the author is "attacked" by a ladder.

CLOSING REMARKS

Thanks for accompanying me up to this point and for learning with me. Learning is an important process that never ends. I, too, learned a lot by trying to teach you the basics of the Modular System in a form that is new to me.

I hope I have been able to give you insight into defense with a knife. Surely there are still a lot of open questions. I can only encourage you to go on the search for answers. Quite often, these answers are not right in front of your nose. I, too, often have to spend long hours in an airplane to get answers. But if your search leads you to us, you are welcome in our seminars. Surely you will find more answers here.

While on the search, don't let yourself be impressed by martial appearance. Slitting open bellies and lots of blood are not the goal and are mostly a facade. I have met women as well as men whom I don't want to have as an enemy in any second of my life. Most probably it will never come to this, because those people are very friendly, helpful, emphatic, and calm.

The knowledge about options for defense with a knife should in any case be accompanied by a positive shaping of personality. Always be aware of the enormous responsibility resting on you when having more capabilities than others.

This book was written for those who want to defend themselves in accordance with the law. For all the others it won't be of use anyway. And that's a good thing.

OTHER SCHIFFER BOOKS ON RELATED TOPICS

KNIFEMAKING FOR BEGINNERS

By: Stefan Steigerwald & Dirk Burmester
ISBN: 978-0-7643-5734-3

The best way to start in knifemaking is usually to make a fixed-blade knife, and this photo-rich guide gives carefully detailed instructions for a full tang knife and a hidden tang knife. Make each of these knives by following the individual construction principles here, and learn all phases of the knifemaking process.

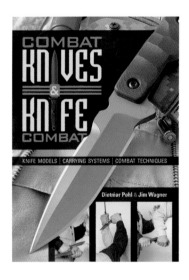

COMBAT KNIVES AND KNIFE COMBAT

By: Dietmar Pohl & Jim Wagner
ISBN: 978-0-7643-4834-1

A comprehensive compendium with respect to all aspects of self-defense knives: history and development, technology, practice, training and combat techniques.